Ce

INTERNATIONAL STUDIES

The Origins of Polish Socialism

INTERNATIONAL STUDIES

PUBLISHED FOR THE CENTRE FOR
INTERNATIONAL STUDIES, LONDON SCHOOL OF
ECONOMICS AND POLITICAL SCIENCE

The Centre for International Studies at the London
School of Economics was established in 1967 with
the aid of a grant from the Ford Foundation. Its
aim is to promote research and advanced training
on a multi-disciplinary basis in the general field of
International Studies, particular emphasis being
given initially to contemporary China, the Soviet
Union and Eastern Europe and the relationship
between these areas and the outside world. To this
end the Centre offers research fellowships and
studentships and, in collaboration with other bodies
(such as the Social Science Research Council),
sponsors research projects and seminars.

The Centre is undertaking a series of publications
in International Studies, of which this volume is the
first.

Whilst the Editorial Board accepts responsibility for recom-
mending the inclusion of a volume in the series, the author is
alone responsible for the views and opinions expressed.

THE ORIGINS OF
POLISH SOCIALISM

THE HISTORY AND IDEAS OF
THE FIRST POLISH SOCIALIST
PARTY 1878–1886

LUCJAN BLIT

*Lecturer in Political Institutions of Eastern Europe in the
Department of Government at the London School of
Economics and the Department of History of the School of
Slavonic and East European Studies, at the University
of London*

CAMBRIDGE

AT THE UNIVERSITY PRESS 1971

Published by the Syndics of the Cambridge University Press
Bentley House, 200 Euston Road, London N.W.1
American Branch: 32 East 57th Street, New York, N.Y.10022

© Cambridge University Press 1971

Library of Congress Catalogue Card Number: 70–152642

ISBN: 0 521 08192 0

Printed in Great Britain
by Alden & Mowbray Ltd
at the Alden Press, Oxford

CONTENTS

PREFACE

The Poles are a historically minded nation. They remember that between the fifteenth and the seventeeth centuries Poland was one of the great empires of Europe. Their Kings' writ then ran beyond their eastern and northern boundaries. Since that time the Poles have never looked on their neighbours as equals, either in politics or in culture. They remember, too, the four partitions of their state between 1772 and 1939. These national catastrophes gave rise to a widespread and deeply felt animosity towards their larger neighbours, which the occupation régimes of the Second World War reinforced. It is therefore natural that to many the history of the Poles in modern times is the history of noble and uncomplicated patriotism.

Polish poets, writers and artists were the prophets and flag-bearers of this patriotism. Adam Mickiewicz, Juliusz Słowacki and Frederick Chopin in the nineteenth century, Cyprian Norwid and Stefan Żeromski in the twentieth century, were the spokesmen of the nation, no less than the most famous political and military leaders of the last two centuries: Tadeusz Kościuszko or Józef Pilsudski.

Yet there was also another strand in Polish political thought. In July 1944 a new régime began to be established in Poland. Its most charactcristic political mark was a declaration of total loyalty and even of devotion on the part of the leaders of the new régime towards Russia. Since then a permanent attachment to the Soviet state has remained the basis of People's Poland's foreign and even internal policies. This has appeared to many as completely new in Polish history.

The lack of a free and unfettered forum for Polish public opinion must leave open the question how far the political ruling class represents the real feelings of the people on this matter. But it would be a mistake to assume that a pro-Russian foreign policy is contrary to everything in the Polish past. During the nineteenth century more than one prominent and patriotic figure among the Poles tried, although in vain, to find some kind of *modus vivendi* between his nation and the Russian Tsars. From the beginning of the twentieth century until 1917 (when first one and then a second revolution made the Russians unacceptable to the right wing in Polish politics) a strong popular movement pursued the same line under the leadership of Roman Dmowski.

Quite a few of those who now rule Poland as communists are emotionally and even intellectually close to the tradition of the now formally extinct Polish National Democrats. But even the more orthodox marxists among them can look back to the tradition of Polish–Russian friendship and collaboration. This was the tradition of the majority of Polish marxists. The early Russian revolutionaries, and later the marxists of the Social Democratic party (Mensheviks and Bolsheviks), were for them their natural comrades-in-arms with whose help and under whose leadership the Russia of the Tsars was to be transformed into the Russian republic of victorious socialism.

This book tells the story of the pioneers of Polish marxism and international socialism. They lived and were politically active in the later seventies and early eighties of the last century. Although hunted by the Tsarist police, who in the end succeeded in liquidating both their organisation and most of their members, they left many documents which enable us to understand how they viewed themselves and what they thought of those with whom they disagreed and against whom they fought. This book is based mainly on the manifestos, political tracts and the three periodicals which they published during their short period of activity. Of great additional help has been the documentation of their activities prepared by the gendarmerie for the Third Department in St Petersburg which was watching revolutionary movements in the Russian empire. Another source was the memoirs of those of its leaders and members who escaped the gallows and survived Siberia, or who were lucky enough to avoid arrest and find an asylum in the more liberal West.

The present book is the first part of a larger work on which I am engaged. My aim is to write the history of the Polish marxist movement up to its present days of power and deep ideological crisis.

This book could not have been written without the help of the Centre for International Studies at the London School of Economics and Political Science where I held a Research Fellowship from October 1968 to December 1969.

Professors Leonard Schapiro and Geoffrey Goodwin, both of the London School of Economics, and Mr Henry T. Willetts of St Antony's College, Oxford, kindly read my manuscript before publication and made valuable comments which helped me to avoid some mistakes of fact and interpretation. I am most grateful to them. But I alone am responsible for any wrong opinion or mistake the reader may find in this book.

I want also gratefully to acknowledge the help of the British Library of Political and Economic Science who allowed me to quote documents of Ludwik Waryński, Stanisław Kunicki and Piotr Bardovsky belonging to the Wojnicz Collection in their possession. I want also to thank the Internationaal Instituut voor Sociale Geschiedenis in Amsterdam whose Director kindly permitted the reproduction of letters written by members of the party concerning the movement.

Last but not least I want to express my thanks to Mrs Marion Horn of the Centre for International Studies who gave generously of her time and skill to prepare my manuscript for publication. And this is no less true of my wife who read the manuscript when it was still in preparation.

LUCJAN BLIT

February 1971

1 THE DEFEATED PAST

On 22 January 1863 the conspiratorial Central National Committee called the Polish nation to rise against the Tsar.

This was to prove to be the last battle in the long struggle for Polish independence led, and mostly fought, by the gentry. The long struggle had begun in 1795 in defence of the patriotic constitution of 3 May 1791, under the leadership of the noblest representative of that class, Tadeusz Kościuszko. The magnates, the great landlords and their hangers-on had by their anarchic behaviour brought about two partitions of the Republic. The democratic gentry saw themselves as the only class which could achieve the resurrection of Poland. They would enlarge the nation to include its overwhelming majority, the peasantry (and also, as some said, the Jews in the towns). Their proud slogan throughout the nineteenth century was: 'Z polską szlachtą polski lud' ('with the Polish gentry are the Polish people').

The Kościuszko insurrection was defeated by the Tsar's bigger armies. Later, the same generation (although not Kościuszko himself who, as a good republican, distrusted the ambitious Emperor) gathered round Napoleon, only to see their hopes shattered again by the defeat of his Russian campaign of 1812.

On 29 November 1830 their sons, the alumni of the Warsaw Officer Cadet School, again proclaimed the independence of the Kingdom of Poland, the product of the Congress of Vienna, 1815. They saw the July revolution of that year in Paris as the long awaited beginning of a Europe of independent nations. This time it took the Tsar's armies more than ten months to reconquer Poland.

In 1863 some of the next generation of the Polish gentry again left their homes for the battle fields. But this time defeat was inevitable. In the Kościuszko insurrection of 1795, during the fifteen years of the Napoleonic wars, and in the 1830–1 insurrection, the patriots had had at their disposal regular Polish armies, which, led by professional officers and in possession of arms as efficient as those of their adversaries, could hope, even though smaller in numbers, to defeat the enemy. But in 1863 they had to fight as guerillas. When the 1863 insurrection started, the Polish National Committee could call on at most some ten thousand badly equipped, scattered and mostly untrained men.[1] They were opposed by the Russian garrisons on Polish soil comprising a hundred thousand soldiers, who could always call on huge reserves in Russia proper.

From the very beginning the insurgents suffered from a feeling of deadly isolation. The promise of the Central National Committee, the political command centre of the uprising, to free the peasants from servitude and to give them equal legal and political rights in a future independent Poland awoke no real response in the villages. And even among the younger members of the gentry or the better-off urban population the call to battle was often ignored or even rejected. The young Warsaw University, the *Szkoła Główna*, refused to take part. Only thirteen of the 728 undergraduate students joined the partisan groups. According to secret Russian police reports seventy-three others were 'politically compromised', or sympathisers with the national cause.[2]

As usual in such cases the best suffered most; the most idealistic formed the vanguard of the patriots, and were annihilated. Those taken prisoner by the Russian armies were considered 'rebels' and either executed on the spot, or sent to Siberia to hard labour in the mines. A historian of this period gave the figure of 30,000 as the number of Poles who died in the battles of 1863–5. Official executions were given as 396; 3,399 persons were sentenced to penal servitude (*Katorga*); 6,959 young men were sent to penal army units and 18,673 were exiled to Siberia either for life or for very long periods.[3]

In an uneven struggle the Polish nation, or that part of it which lived under the Tsars, lost its most culturally and politically valuable members. The patriotic fortresses of the nation, the houses of the middle and small gentry, were looted, sometimes burned down, often confiscated. Of the active young patriots, most at the end were either dead, in exile, or in hiding. This was a great enough disaster. Worse was to come.

In March 1864 the Russian imperial government published a decree freeing the Polish peasants from their servitude and from other obligations towards the land-owners.[4] This decree went much further than that which had emancipated the peasants in Russia proper in 1861. It gave the peasants on Polish (and also Lithuanian and partly Ukrainian) territory full possession of the land they had until then rented. The amount of land assigned to a Polish peasant farm was, on average, four times as large as that received by a Russian peasant.[5] The dream of generations of Polish peasants seemed fulfilled; yet their benefactors were not Poles, but Russian officials acting in the name of the Tsar.

The defeats the patriotic bands suffered in the field were highly painful, but predictable. The new mood of hostility which the partisans encountered from the Polish peasantry was a political and psychological catastrophe. One Polish historian characterised the situation thus: 'The peasant mass at once turned away from the uprising.'[6] Another[7] described how peasants attacked insurgents in southern Poland when they fled from the pursuing Russian soldiers, and handed them over to the enemy. A contemporary wrote in his memoirs about whole insurgent units being massacred by 'some thousands of peasants'.[8]

The Tsarist government skilfully exploited the age-old divergence of interest between the peasantry and the land-owning classes. The fight for an independent Polish state was presented as a war of greedy men who wanted to keep their possessions intact; as the action of the oppressors of the peasants whose only true friend and defender was the Emperor of Russia. While the insurrection was bleeding to death, 'a deputation of Polish peasants was received with honours in St Petersburg in 1864, and Secretary of State Platanov addressed them in the Tsar's name, thanking them for their loyalty'.[9]

Many peasants were executed by the outraged partisans. This only deepened the wounds, which took two generations to heal.

The uprising of 1863–4 closed the chapter of Polish history in which the patriotic middle and small gentry fought a heroic but forlorn battle for an independent Poland. They had on their side the sympathies of most of liberal Europe. They won the support of the emerging new socialist movement. But they were dangerously isolated in their own country. The majority of their compatriots were either neutral or openly hostile. Many who had fought and been defeated were in despair. Was this Finis Poloniae?

To survive, the nation had to find fresh ideas, another outlook, new horizons.

THE CHANGING SOCIETY

The emancipation of the Polish peasants in 1864 was no doubt the most important historical event in Poland during the nineteenth century. It profoundly changed the economic and social structure of society. It had long-lasting political consequences. Less than forty years later a great Polish poet, Stanisław Wyspiański (and poetry in Poland since the beginning of the nineteenth century has been mainly about politics), would announce in 'The Wedding': 'The peasant is mighty, that is all.'

But even before the radical agrarian reform was introduced by the Russian government as a successful counteraction against the patriotic gentry, the industrial revolution belatedly reached Poland. As everywhere else in Europe it created or increased two urban classes – the workers and the bourgeoisie.

The industrial revolution started in the Russian-ruled Kingdom of Poland in the forties. In 1845 the first railway line was built linking Warsaw with Skierniewice.[10] The decision of Britain in 1842 to lift its embargo on the export of machines was another important factor which accelerated the change from a mostly agricultural to a mixed type of economy in Poland. Another decision which made the changes possible was that of the Russian Government in 1859 to abolish the customs frontier between the Kingdom of Poland and the rest of the Russian empire. The Crimean War (1854–6) was a further element in the growth of industry in the Kingdom of Poland. Russia was then undergoing a severe sea blockade and naturally was vitally interested in supplying her needs with products such as textiles manufactured in the Kingdom of Poland.

The agrarian reform of 1864 created the labour market necessary for the growth and development of the industrial sector in the economy of the Kingdom. It provided the middle and better-off peasants with their own land, the dream of generations. But by the same token it freed tens of thousands of the village labourers from the legal restrictions which had prevented them from looking for a better life in the growing towns and cities. At the same time it was a death blow to many smallholdings of the impoverished gentry.[11] The uprising of 1863–4 only worsened their economic situation. After its defeat, the survivors had to seek for new sources of support for themselves, and their families, and often migrated to the towns. A few of them succeeded in forming the new bourgeoisie. Others, especially the young, formed the growing class of professional people: lawyers, doctors, journalists, engineers and civil servants. The poorest went to work in factories. Their cultural background singled them out from the illiterate mass of the new proletariat, who had just arrived from the villages. The sons of the impoverished but literate gentry, as one would expect, soon came to occupy the posts of skilled and semi-skilled workers or foremen. Among men and women of this background, militant socialism, influenced by the heroism of Russian revolutionary Populists ('Narodnaya Volya') and the growing strength of the Western marxist movements (mainly the German Social Democratic Party), was to find its leaders and followers, its martyrs and its traitors.

The living and working conditions of the new Polish proletariat were miserable. The Russian Governor of Warsaw, Lieutenant-General N. N. Medem, had this to say about the inhabitants of Warsaw working-class suburbs:[12]

Here squeezed into stinking dwellings are living the marginal and most miserable part of Warsaw's working class, hopeless and near to despair. Persons who on my order have on Saturday and Sunday visited some dwellings of these unfortunate people, paint in the most dark colours what they have seen: nearly naked children, who leave their holes only at night time because of lack of clothing; whole families who have not eaten for days, whose adult members loudly express their anger; who openly threaten to repeat the disturbances of 13 and 14 [25–6] of December.[13]

The working day was never less than 11 hours long, but in the textile industry, which in the second half of the nineteenth century employed more workers than any other, the working day lasted 12–14 hours.[14] The normal working week was six days, but Sunday working and overtime were compulsory. As in any other country passing through the birth pangs of the industrial revolution, wages were just enough to keep body and soul together. As soon as the children in a Polish working-class family reached the age of eight, they, like their mother, joined their father in the mill or the mine, thus to supplement his meagre wage packet.

It would be wrong to think that the only ones to feel outraged by the situation were the revolutionary socialists. The Polish newspapers of this period, although heavily censored by the Tsarist authorities, and generally strongly opposed to any socialist ideas, frequently reported on the misery of the new working classes, and demanded reforms. Bolesław Prus, the Polish Charles Dickens, while condemning any thought of radical political action, described in his books and essays with great compassion the sufferings of the poor. But this was sympathy without practical consequences. An additional social complication was the fact that very often foreigners, who did not even speak or understand Polish, occupied the most prominent position in the Polish industrial revolution. At the end of the nineteenth century foreign capital made up 39 per cent of the whole industrial capital in the Kingdom; it owned 25 per cent of all factories; employed 55 per cent of the country's working force and produced 60 per cent of industrial output.[15] The population was growing rapidly. Between the uprising of 1863 and the end of the century it nearly doubled (to 9,402,000). Warsaw's population numbered 243,000 in 1865, but more than 638,000 in the late nineties. From 4,000 inhabitants in the middle of the century, Łódź, the textile centre, exploded to 315,000. The industrial working class rose from a few thousands to 311,000. 600,000 labourers were employed in agriculture. Another 237,000 manual workers were employed in smaller workshops, municipal undertakings, etc.[16] The percentage of industrial workers in Poland was 50 per cent higher than in the population of the rest of Russia.[17]

The industrial explosion in the Kingdom of Poland can best be illustrated by three figures. In 1857 the value of industrial production was 42.5 million roubles, in 1871 it was 66.7 million roubles, fourteen years later, in 1885, it was already 186 million roubles; that is to say, it nearly trebled in less than 15 years.[18]

From being a two-class nation until the middle of the nineteenth century, in less than two decades the Kingdom became, like the rest of central and western Europe, a much more socially complicated modern society, with new economic and political problems of great complexity. But being the country of a suppressed, yet historically conscious, nation made all the normal problems of a young industrial society ten times more intricate, and sometimes even tragic.

'NO MORE DREAMS, GENTLEMEN'

The catastrophe of 1863 was the most painful of all the political and physical defeats suffered by the Polish nation since it had been partitioned at the end of the eighteenth century. After the uprising of 1830–1 many European governments, and especially those of France and Britain, considered it their duty to protect those Poles who had escaped. The Tsar was pressed by powerful governments to preserve some autonomy for his Polish subjects. Nothing of this kind happened after the 1863 insurrection. European political complications concentrated the minds of their governments on other matters. Here and there small groups of radical liberals, or socialists, declared their solidarity with the Poles. The Tsar's government took little notice of them.

After the 1831 campaign 70,000 Polish soldiers left the country for the West.[19] In France, in Britain and in Switzerland, they formed their own political, cultural and self-help organisations, with an elected representation which was recognised and respected by the governments of the Western nations. Their leaders were listened to by prime ministers and foreign secretaries. The Polish cause was an international one.

This exodus in 1831 became known in Polish history as the Great Emigration. It included the most famous names in Polish politics, and military art. But it was even more memorable because of the role played by the great romantic poets and musicians. What they wrote soon returned to the homeland, and became a source of hope and strength. Free Poland lived physically on the Seine and the Thames, but was spiritually one with those who remained in Warsaw, Cracow, Wilno and Poznań.

Not so after 1864. A few thousand insurgents escaped abroad. They arrived without organisation, agreed political aims or leadership. A few joined the small circle of the leaders of the International Workers' Association (better known as the First International). They were to fight in 1871 on the barricades of Paris, as commanders and soldiers of the Commune (100 Poles gave their lives there).[20] But politically they were a shattered assortment of individuals.

'Point de rêveries' – no more dreams, Tsar Alexander II told a delegation of Polish nobles in 1857. Some of them were ready even then to give up all thought of an independent Polish state, but until 1863 they were only a small minority among the politically conscious members of the nation. After 1864 the dreamers were either dead, in exile or too shocked to be able to continue as before. The class which was the main spring of patriotic movements in the nineteenth century, the gentry, saw its position shattered. The overwhelming majority of the nation, the peasants, were, if not actively helping the Russian soldiery to round up the 'rebels', at best completely indifferent. Kazimierz Krzywicki, who in the years preceding the 1863 uprising contributed so greatly to the rebuilding of a modern Polish educational system, published a pamphlet soon after the insurrection, in which he stated that it was utter nonsense to believe that the peasant would ever consider himself a Pole. He therefore advised his compatriots to abandon for ever the idea of leading a national life independent of Russia; on the contrary, only by being loyal to the Tsar could the Poles achieve full rights as the Emperor's subjects.[21]

For a while the centre of political thinking among the Poles moved to more placid Galicia. The gentry were there the undisputed rulers not only of Polish society but of the whole province. Conditions for the preservation of Polish culture, and many institutions, were incomparably more congenial there than in Tsarist Russia or even in Prussia. The slaughter of Polish gentry by Polish peasants in the unsuccessful insurrection of 1846 had not been forgotten. Now, in the shadow of the defeat of the 1863 uprising a movement arose against *Liberum Conspiro*, the century-old habit of patriotic conspiracy for the resurrection of an independent Polish state. Many of those young sons of the upper classes who in 1863 had collected funds and recruited volunteers now began publishing most violent accusations against the leaders and followers of the uprising. A veteran of the 1830 insurrection and one of the most influential political thinkers in Cracow, Paweł Popiel, published an open letter in which he condemned any thought of an armed national uprising or the acceptance of leadership coming from a political emigration.[22] Cracow became the centre of Polish conservatism, preaching loyalty to and collaboration with the partitioning powers. This attitude survived until 1918. It was successful in making possible a very great degree of national autonomy for the Poles in Galicia. The Polish upper classes not only dominated the province but played a prominent role in the politics of imperial Vienna. Their loyalty to the Austrian crown made sense.

But what was possible in the Austro-Hungarian Empire was not applicable in the political conditions of Tsarist Russia. The bureaucracy in St Petersburg had neither the imagination nor the intelligence to play its part in a movement to conciliate the Poles. The 1863 uprising led to a hostile reaction against the Poles even among the groups of liberal Russians (Alexander Herzen being an exception). The Polish aristocracy tried more than once to appease the government in St Petersburg. In 1877 it sent its addresses of loyalty and support for the throne on the eve of the Russo-Turkish War, and again, three years later, when the twenty-fifth anniversary of Alexander II's accession to the throne was celebrated. But to no avail. Count Muraviev, the man who mercilessly suppressed the uprising (he is known in Polish history as the 'hangman'), was the symbol of Russian policy in the Polish Kingdom. There was no place for collaboration, even for the most docile loyalists. Russification of the ten million Poles became the goal. In 1868 Russian was made the teaching language in all gymnasia (secondary schools). A year later the administration closed the Polish University in Warsaw and opened instead a Russian University. The Roman Catholic Church paid dearly for the sympathy which many of its lower clergy had shown for the insurgents. In 1867 the Russian government forbade it to have any relations with the Vatican. A specially created council, sitting in St Petersburg, supervised its activities.

The Russian viceroy, Count Theodor Berg, abolished the Polish administrative system and introduced a new one, based on the Russian *gubernia*. He brought from Russia proper thousands of not very subtle or experienced bureaucrats, and removed Poles from any positions of responsibility or influence in local government.

But although the losses in human terms were heavy, the fact that no political emigration followed the military and political defeat of the insurrection was of immense consequence. It freed the Poles from illusions and false hopes. Secret emissaries bringing the good news that a foreign emperor or a political potentate was on the verge of offering help for the resurrection of the Fatherland were no longer expected to arrive. The nation had to find its own answers to the great question: how to survive and retain its identity when devoid of a state organisation and political power?

The alumni of the *Szkoła Główna* turned their eyes to the West: to Britain and France. They assiduously read, and translated into Polish, the works of Darwin, Comte, John Stuart Mill, Spencer and, later, Marx. Those who studied them were nearly all the sons of the land-owning gentry. Their past lay in ruins. The Western philosophers, anthropologists, economists and sociologists opened new horizons and new hopes for them.

Their language was not, as in the years of the Great Emigration, that of emotion. They appealed to reason, they sought reality. No more for these young Poles the call of the poet, Adam Mickiewicz, to 'measure strength according to the goal'. They would no longer play Sisyphus against the rolling Russian stone. They had to find a new and realistic basis for the future existence both of the nation, and of themselves. But this was not enough. To save its culture and its cohesion the nation had to explore every opening which the forced incorporation into the Russian state had produced.

First came the rejection of the past. 'We must then reject the last movement [i.e. uprising], recognise it and condemn it as fatal, thrust away those who led it or who approved of it.'[23] It was not only the political commentators and philosophers who expressed the opinion that 'dreams of recapturing external independence must give way to the endeavour for internal existence'.[24] They were joined by the traditional prophets of the nation, the bards and writers. The poet Adam Asnyk had until 1863 been an enthusiastic upholder of the insurrectionary ideas of the first half of the nineteenth century, and in the final stage of the uprising even became a member of the radical national government under the leadership of Romuald Traugut. But in the later sixties he joined those who turned away from any thought of armed struggle. Another romantic writer, Józef Kraszewski, whose historical novels à la Walter Scott depicted the glorious past of the nation and state, considered the defeat of 1863 the end of the road. The uprisings had not freed the nation. On the contrary, they had brought immense human suffering in their train and in the end endangered the very existence of the people. The Poles had to give up, at least for a time, their notions of an independent state. 'We believe', Kraszewski wrote in 1868, 'in slow and gradual progress [which] through reforming individuals, increasing enlightenment, encouraging work, order and moderation should accomplish the most salutary revolution, or rather evolution of the social system.'[25]

The Western liberal philosophers, economists and political thinkers helped the young members of the Polish intelligentsia to reconsider their ideas of the role of the state in the life of a nation. It was shown to be of secondary importance compared with other values in a liberal society, which could prosper and progress without the intervention of governments. Thus the question of political independence was no longer the nub of their thoughts. Nation and society could be preserved as part of a larger political and economic entity: the Russian empire. The need was to discover the sources needed to revitalise the nation's life. They found these in the speedily developing industry and commerce, which, notwithstanding the losses caused by the insurrection and savage Tsarist repressions, was changing and enriching the economic face of the Kingdom of Poland. In Auguste Comte's Positivist Philosophy they found their bible of rational thought, based on scientific investigation, which had to be followed by imaginative, but not romantic, practical action. They called themselves 'Warsaw Positivists'. For the first time in Polish history the slogan 'enrichissez-vous' could be publicly proclaimed without the fear of being accused of fostering selfish, dishonourable goals. To become successful in business took on the virtue of patriotic achievement. The most able political publicist of this period, himself a product of the *Szkoła Główna*, Alexander Świętochowski, best expressed the feelings and aspiration of the Warsaw Positivists when he wrote: 'We ought not to expect anything [positive] from political revolutions, wars, international agreements, changeable favours from strangers; but let us trust our own vitality. Let us occupy any evacuated positions, let us squeeze into every chink, let us put down roots wherever we can find proper soil.'[26]

But as in any other country experiencing the first phase of an industrial revolution, the optimistic philosophy of a new social class that reaped its great benefits was not shared by those who were sucked from the villages and decaying little market towns into the stinking slums of the rising industrial cities and settlements. While the ideas of the Warsaw Positivists found a sympathetic echo among many of the sons of the ruined gentry who were being recruited into the growing number of managerial posts, and who henceforward could consider their work for the

new bourgeoisie (often of German and Jewish origin) as completely in accord with their patriotic honour, others, members of
the same social class, rejected this stage of development with
disgust. One of them later described the feelings of this second
group thus: 'The first socialist movement in Warsaw [in the
seventies of the nineteenth century] was...a heartfelt reaction
against the bourgeois slogans of organic work, against the atrophe
of every political thought, against the mean theory of soul-less
"indicators" and a still more base practice.'[27]

Warsaw Positivism and Polish marxism were the main ideas of
the new society which took the place of the Poland of the gentry,
whose last honourable fight for the leadership of the nation had
been shattered in 1863. Both rejected, at least in theory, any
sentiment which was not based on rational thinking or which was
contrary to scientific truth. Yet each of them considered the other
as either base and vulgar or as unrealistic and wrongheaded. As
Alexander Świętochowski wrote in a newspaper a few days after
the first socialist programme was being clandestinely printed and
distributed in Warsaw: 'Socialism until today is a fantastic
building constructed out of scientific mist, of charitable illusions,
from human misery's dreams.'[28]

It would be wrong to think that the Warsaw Positivists, who
saw in the development of industry and agriculture the golden
key to the future of the Poles, who highly praised every manifestation of private economic initiative, and considered material
advance a great national and personal virtue, were blind to the
sufferings of the disinherited villagers who in Warsaw, Łódź or
Sosnowiec led the miserable life of the new proletariat. The
Warsaw Positivist newspapers of this period were full of realistic
descriptions of the lamentable conditions in which the workers
and their families had to live. The same papers also reported the
new progressive regulations and laws which were being introduced
in England, Germany and France to protect the workers.

One of the most prominent writers of this time, Bolesław
Prus-Głowacki, also a firm believer in bourgeois virtue, devoted
much of his talent to pricking the conscience of the newly rich in
respect of the slum dwellers in the suburbs and industrial

settlements. But in the eyes of the young socialists the Positivists, the enthusiasts of 'organic work', were little better, if not worse, than the Russian 'tchinovniks'. Moreover, this enemy was at home, in the smart quarters of the city, in the office of the factory director. He was easier to engage, or so it seemed to the first Polish socialists. The gap between the living standard of the bourgeoisie and the dispossessed was enormous. The newly rich not only wanted to enjoy their wealth but also to flaunt it. Most of them had not the social prestige of a good family background. The conditions existing in the Russia of Alexander II precluded any political advance. A few went in for public patronage and helped to establish good schools or art museums. But most enjoyed their affluence without bothering too much about the way the 'lower classes' lived.

The situation was ideal for a marxist interpretation of society. The exploitation was plain for everyone to see. The class differences were obvious. Apart from the primitive labour relations existing between the employer and his workers, there were no other links binding them together. The conditions which gave birth to marxist revolutionary movements in other parts of Europe were fast maturing in the Kingdom of Poland. And just as with most marxist movements in other countries, so too among the Poles it was not the workers, not the proletarians, but the sons and daughters of the higher social groups who were to be the propagators and organisers of the revolutionary class struggle.

2 A NEW GENERATION

THE SOCIALIST STUDENTS

'In this land of tombs the fire has died down', wrote the Polish poet, Kornel Ujejski, after the defeat of 1863.

The Warsaw Positivists, the advocates of prosaic 'organic work', appealed to those who made a profit by selling cheap Białystok textiles to the Russian peasant in Vyatka; who were content to look after their families, collect the green rouble banknotes, and to go abroad to 'take the waters'.

Later a prominent group of Polish artists was to turn to the nation's past, to write books and paint pictures in an effort to 'uplift the people's spirit'. The novels of Henryk Sienkiewicz and the paintings of Jan Mateyko played a big role in saving the post-insurrection generation of young Poles from dissolving into cultural nihilism or succumbing to a soulless careerism.

But for the moment apathy, only slightly camouflaged by quotations from Comte and Spencer, reigned in the Kingdom.

It was very different in Russia proper. There the Populist movement of 'going to the people' fascinated the young of the educated classes, and challenged the divine right of the Tsar autocratically to rule his hundred and twenty million subjects. As never before, Russian society immersed itself in a wide-ranging debate about the way in which it would like to be re-created. Western ideas, merged with Russian thought, were presented by a great number of passionate and often highly original writers. Some of them, like Alexander Herzen, published their books and articles abroad. But many more appeared with the imprint of St Petersburg or Moscow. The government decree of 1865 freeing books from preventive censorship contributed greatly to the intellectual and political thaw of this period. 'It was stagnation with us while Russia was on the move', sadly remarked a Polish Socialist historian who wrote about these years.[1] While intellectual life in Russia was flowering, while the universities in St Petersburg, Moscow and Kiev became centres where young educated men during endless talks and debates sharpened their minds on new ideas, the heavy hand of the Russian 'tchinovnik' stifled every sign of spiritual life in the Kingdom of Poland. As mentioned before, the Polish University in Warsaw, *Szkoła Główna*, the only one in the Kingdom, was closed by a Tsarist decree. The authorities regarded it as an obstacle to their policy of russification, although its pupils had opposed the insurrection before 1863, and condemned the very idea of armed rebellion against the Tsar in the years after the uprising. Indeed it was from Russia itself that modern ideas of socialism, marxism and revolution reached the Kingdom of Poland in the seventies of the last century. Yet they were seldom 'pure' Russian. They soon mixed or merged with socialist ideas from Geneva, Paris, Vienna, and Berlin. But no historian of the modern Polish socialist movement can deny the influence which revolutionary and socialist ideas originating in Russia had on intellectuals, and workers in Warsaw, Łódź and Wilno, and even Cracow.

We have mentioned as reasons for this phenomenon the fact that while the Poles lay prostrate after the bloodletting of 1863–4, Russia was in the midst of a great intellectual and political upheaval. A second reason was the great influx of young Poles into Russian universities. As was only to be expected, they were nearly all the sons (and a very few, daughters) of the gentry. A very few, some of them Jews, were the children of the new bourgeoisie. Generally, they did not come from the central parts of the Kingdom, where this class was morally and materially ruined. Their fathers saw no future for their children in staying on the land, and they would gladly have prepared them for a new profession such as medicine or engineering;[2] but in most cases they lacked the financial means to do so. It was otherwise with the Polish gentry in the Ukraine and in Volynia. They had been spared the brutal suppression of the Poles in the Kingdom or in Lithuania. Their land had seldom been confiscated. As frontiersmen they were more accustomed to the changing moods of human fate. They had fought more often than other Poles against their eastern neighbour. But they also knew him more intimately. Most of them knew the Russian language and some Russian literature. They knew that the Universities of St Petersburg or Moscow were not only places of learning but that radical ideas were there conquering the minds of the young. They did not mind. One of the Polish students of St Petersburg University at this time wrote that when the father of Kazimierz Dłuski, who became a pioneer first of marxism and later of the patriotic Polish socialist movement, discovered his son's revolutionary activities, he said with disapproval, 'You will smash your heads', and then handed him over a thousand roubles, which paid for the first Polish socialist publications.[3]

Feliks Kon, who played a leading role in the 'Proletariat', remarked in his memoirs:[4]

The Polish youth in the east which was attending Russian educational institutes found itself in a much better situation [than the emerging working class in Poland]. This youth came into constant contact with young Russian revolutionaries. It is therefore no surprise that as a result after 1874 there emerged in Russian University cities groups of Polish revolutionaries, who in the beginning participated in the Russian revolutionary movement, and later led the revolutionary activities in Poland.

A historian of this time wrote:[5]

Among the Polish youth [in the Russian Universities] in this epoch a socialist community springs up. Two roads, two possibilities are open to them. Some consider it to be their aim and duty directly to participate in the Russian socialist movement. The spokesman of this group is Ignacy Hrynie-wiecki, a student of the Technological Institute [situated in St Petersburg, this Institute became a centre of Russian marxism]. Others take the position that their task is to return home and there to lay the foundations of socialism among the Polish toiling masses. Naturally this division is not strict. There will be those who will simultaneously find themselves in the Russian and Polish movements, as for example, Stanisław Kunicki. But this also cor-responds to the evolutionary tendencies of the organisational life. At first the socialism of Polish youth finds expression by joining Russian organisations, afterwards it takes the form of founding separate organisations of Polish socialist youth.

Some of the young Polish revolutionaries were so attracted by the Russian movements and intellectual life that they stopped thinking of themselves as Poles. This was true even of some future leaders of the 'Proletariat', such as Stanisław Kunicki (who was born in Georgia of a Polish father and a Georgian mother). On the other hand, Ignacy Hryniewiecki, who as a member of the' Narodnaya Volya' on 13 March (1 March according to the Russian calendar) 1881 assassinated Alexander II, when asked by other Poles why he refused to join their revolutionary groups said: 'When you will go into the forests [as guerillas] I will be with you but as long as you do nothing I will be working for the liberation of Russia.'[6]

The ideological development then taking place in the Russian revolutionary movement after the Narodniki split into the terrorist 'Narodnaya Volya' and the group known as 'Tschorny Peredyel', which considered socialist propaganda among workers as the indispensable condition of a victorious revolution in Russia, exerted a great influence on the ideological evolution of the first Polish socialist groups in Russia. Ironically, it was the Russians who forced them to reconsider their attitude to an independent state life for Poland. 'Narodnaya Volya' declared uncompromisingly that 'the nations incorporated into the Russian state have the right to break away or to remain in the general association'.[7]

In 1880 the separate groups of Polish socialist students in St Petersburg formed a united revolutionary centre which they called 'Gmina Socyalistów Polskich' (the Polish Socialist Commune; this was the traditional name of Polish socialist groups which had emerged among the emigrés of the 1830–1 insurrection, who had settled in Britain). It spread to the universities of Moscow, Kiev and Vilno, where similar communes came into being. But its main interest was in Poland. It concentrated on sending its most prominent members to Poland to strengthen the small groups of socialists in Warsaw; it formed the idea of founding a Polish party. The leadership of the Socialist Revolutionary Party 'Proletariat' consisted overwhelmingly of former students of the Russian universities. It is therefore no surprise to find that many ideas which matured among Russian revolutionaries were taken up by at least a part of Polish socialism.

But even before the St Petersburg Polish Socialist Commune came into being, the emissaries of Polish student groups in

Russia penetrated the newly refounded Warsaw University. At first their socialist pleading was rejected by the majority of those who came to their clandestine meetings, who were under the influence of the Warsaw Positivists and who condemned socialism as contrary to the scientific laws governing the economic and social life of modern nations; and also because of the obvious Russian influence.[8] But very soon the mood at Warsaw University started to change radically. In the years 1877–9 socialist groups among the Polish students in Warsaw were the best organised. They led an active life and attracted the best brains. They were the centre not only of socialist discussions but also of active resistance against the ruthless policy of russification in the field of higher education, implemented by the heavy-handed Tsarist Curator of the Warsaw Educational District, Alexander Apukhtin. The socialist students were strong enough in the early eighties to persuade a majority of departmental delegates to decide to use the money collected for the four hundredth anniversary of the astronomer Nicolas Copernicus for the publication of Karl Marx's works.[9]

The Tsarist authorities were very early worried about the influence of socialist and revolutionary ideas among the Poles. As early as the middle of 1873 (24 August) the third section of the Imperial Chancellory wrote in a memorandum to Alexander II: 'Of all lands belonging to his Imperial Majesty the Kingdom of Poland more than any other constitutes a favourable ground for the Internationale.'[10]

LUDWIK WARYŃSKI

The pioneers of Polish socialism and marxism were small in number and very young in age. Most of them were no more than twenty years old when they became active in, and sometimes the leaders of, the conspiratorial groups, circles and committees. Most of them died early, some on the Tsar's gallows, others in prisons or in Siberian exile. A few committed suicide either because they could bear their sufferings no longer or because disillusion and despair followed the years of great hopes and excitement.

They were brave and often very able. Sons and daughters of a shattered class and a defeated nation, they challenged their own apathetic society and declared war, politically and physically, on the mighty Russia of the Tsars.

They had not much time to study, to think, or to work out their ideas. At the time of the arrests, and their disappearance from public life either for ever or for decades, Ludwik Waryński, the oldest among them, was only 26 years old; Alexander Dębski was 25, Stanisław Kunicki 24, Tadeusz Rechniewski and Edmund Płoski were 21 and Feliks Kon only 20. The exception was the Russian Piotr Bardovsky, Justice of the Peace in Warsaw, who was 40 when he was hanged, together with three other members of the 'Proletariat'. Among the less prominent members of the party, especially among the workers, some were in their thirties and forties. But even then, and for understandable reasons, the young, the unmarried, were the most active. The two workers who were hanged on 28 January 1886 in the Warsaw Citadel (together with Piotr Bardovsky and Stanisław Kunicki) were Michał Ossowski, 23, and Jan Pietrusiński, 22 years old.

Ludwik Waryński contributed more than any of the others to the formation of the International Social Revolutionary Party 'Proletariat'. It was he who gave it an ideology and organisational form. He was its acknowledged leader until his arrest on 28 September 1883. A man of outstanding energy and a brilliant mind, and possessing the charisma which makes a leader of men, he packed into less than six years of his short political life (he died in February 1889 in the severe Tsarist prison in the Shlisselburg fortress at the age of 33) all the drama and tragedy of the first generation of Polish socialists.

Ludwik Waryński's biography is to a very great extent the history of the most decisive period of the formation of Polish marxism. In his few speeches, of which records survive, in his articles published in the Warsaw clandestine magazine *Proletariat* (1883–4), in the memoirs of his Polish and Russian contemporary comrades in arms, he appears as the chief thinker of this group.

From being a follower of Bakunin, and a believer in an imminent social revolution which was to change Europe into a federation of socialist states, he moved to the marxist position of recognising class conflict as the decisive force in modern history. He vehemently rejected the patriotic tradition of the social group, the small gentry, whence he sprang. He was not cosmopolitan, but an outspoken internationalist, and an uncompromising advocate of the need, indeed of the duty, for Polish socialists and revolutionaries organically to collaborate with their Russian comrades.

Waryński's background was very characteristic, and very similar to that of many of the young leaders of the 'Proletariat'.[11] He was born on 24 September 1856 in Martynovka, a Ukraine village in Kanyov *oblast*, which was part of the Kiev *gubernia*. His father, Ludwik-Severyn, graduated in mathematics at Kiev University, and is said to have been active in the 1863 conspiracy. At the time of Ludwik Tadeusz's birth, his father was the tenant of a considerable farm. Martynovka, the village where Ludwik grew up as a *panicz* (young gentleman), had a population of 3,000, of whom only twenty-six were Roman Catholic, into which Church he was baptised. Thus nearly all the people whom he met first in life were Ukrainian-Orthodox. Of the population of the Kanyov *oblast*, 90 per cent belonged to the Orthodox Church; 9 per cent were Jews and only 1 per cent Roman Catholic. Although the Waryńskis were patriotic Poles and loyal Catholics, the fact that Ludwik's playmates were children of a different nationality and religion must have had a strong influence on his future political ideas and attitudes.

The region was far from being purely agricultural. According to an official report published in 1880, apart from farms the *oblast* had thirty-one factories, employing 5,000 workers, mainly in sugar plantations, distilleries and breweries. In the nearby town of Korsun there was a large iron foundry.

In 1865 Ludwik was sent to the gymnasium in Byela Tserkev, a nearby market town with a mixed Ukrainian–Jewish–Polish population.

The school was founded by the Polish magnate Count Branicki and until 1861 was Polish in language and spirit. After 1861 the government proscribed the Polish language, closed the magnificent Polish library, and the Roman Catholic chapel was changed into an Orthodox church. The pupils were forbidden to speak Polish even in private, under the threat of severe punishment. In 1869 Latin was removed from the curriculum as turning the scholars' minds to things Western. Even when a teacher was otherwise liberally minded, as was the case with the school's director, Mikhail Kornyevitch Tchaly, who was later dismissed for delivering a eulogy at the funeral of the Ukrainian poet Schevchenko, he could still be openly hostile to everything Polish (this was a widespread phenomenon in Russia after the 1863 uprising). In such an atmosphere it was only natural that the more sensitive Polish boys came together secretly and in the best national tradition formed a clandestine organisation whose aim was to study the Polish language, poetry and history, to write essays on these subjects, and then collectively to discuss them.[12] It was in this patriotic Polish organisation that the future leader of the antipatriotic faction of Polish marxism got his first training in underground work.

Waryński matriculated in 1874 when he was 18 years old. The impoverished Polish gentry saw no future for their sons on their farms. Ludwik had always been interested in mechanical work, and so he was sent to St Petersburg's Technological Institute, while his younger brother, Stanisław, who went to the same school in Byela Tserkev, chose medicine. The Technological Institute, which was situated in the elegant Zagorodny Prospect, then enjoyed the reputation of having first-class teachers among its professors. But even more important for the future evolution of Waryński was the fact that the Institute was the centre of revolutionary and socialist groups. The strongest among them were the Populists (*Narodniki*). It was characteristic of them that they scorned the Western European practice of constitutional advance. Instead they believed in a millennium when there would be a break in social and economic conditions in Russia, which would result in a radical political change. Not much is known about Waryński's connections with Russian revolutionary groups in the Institute. He himself later joined there a Polish socialist underground group. But as many Poles in the Institute, among them Ignacy Hryniewiecki, the assassin of Alexander II, were active members of 'Narodnaya Volya' or Russian anarchist groups, there can be no doubt that Waryński was at least partly influenced by them. They responded to his deeper nature. Whatever he said later about scientific laws conditioning man's behaviour, he was a romantic at heart. His later marxism always had on it the reflection of the sunny St Petersburg days of anarchistic-populist dreaming. And the later Polish marxists, who declared him their St Peter, had from time to time to exorcise his unorthodox Russian pre-marxist traditions.[13]

Waryński never graduated at the Institute. A few weeks after the beginning of his second year of studies, in November 1875, trouble began. The students at all the colleges of higher education in St Petersburg demanded representation on the disciplinary committees, on the scholarship-awarding boards and in other matters. After a stormy meeting during which the director of the Institute, Vyshnyegradsky, was verbally assaulted by a student, repressions started. Among those suspended was Ludwik Waryński. He was put under police supervision for a year in his father's place of residence. He read, he thought, and he made the choice which ended his active life six years later. He was 20 years old when he began his journey to Warsaw.

3 THE BEGINNING

THE 'PROGRAMME OF POLISH SOCIALISTS' (1878)

When Ludwik Waryński arrived in Warsaw in the first months of 1877 he was warmly received by the members of the small existing groups of socialists. Most of them were either students of Warsaw University or its graduates. Some of the members of the intelligentsia such as Kazimierz Dłuski, Stanisław Mendelson, Kazimierz Puchewicz, Cezaryna Wojnarowska and Szymon Dikstein were to play a most prominent role in the coming years in establishing the Polish socialist movement. Among the members of the first clandestine socialist groups in Warsaw in the later half of the seventies we also find the half-educated sons of the impoverished gentry, Henryk Dulęba, Kazimierz Dąbrowski, Ludwik Kobylański, who joined the working class, and acted as a bridge between the socialist intelligentsia and the first generation of Polish workers, sons of illiterate peasants who had just been freed from serfdom. The socialist groups also had Jewish members. Until then the large Jewish population in the Kingdom of Poland had lived in a spiritual and political ghetto. To break out of it, to be accepted into Polish society, a Jew had not only to become completely assimilated, but also to renounce his religion. One or two did so successfully, like the wealthy industrialist and financier, Leopold Kronenberg, who founded the Technological Institute in Warsaw and who became a leading member of the 'moderates' in the years 1861–4. But it was only in the socialist groups that one could find Jews of very poor origin, like the brilliant propagandist Szymon Dikstein, who were fully accepted as members of a Polish political movement.

The Warsaw socialist groups, or 'circles' as they were called, had no unifying organisation. Their contacts were of a purely personal nature. They needed a man who could centralise their activities and coalesce their ideas. Ludwik Waryński had the analytical brain, the consistency of thought, the pioneering energy and the passion of the born agitator needed for this task. His faith in the new ideas then spreading over Europe, his romantic belief in his duty to lead and to serve, and his youth – he was then only 21 years old – made him impervious to the certain fate that awaited him. He became the leader of the first generation of Polish socialists.

Waryński found the 'propaganda circles' too self-centred. His ambition was to have not only people who understood socialist theory, but active participants in the struggle against the existing conditions. According to all the memoirs written by his contemporaries, who either escaped abroad or survived imprisonment and Siberian exile, Waryński like all the other early Polish socialists believed that his task was to organise the workers (and to a limited extent the peasants also) to fight against their immediate exploiters, the factory owners. This struggle was to achieve two aims at the same time: on the one hand it would immediately improve the miserable conditions in which the first generation of industrial workers in Polish towns and cities were living; on the other hand it would bring about the final collapse of the capitalist system, and the victory of the millennial Social Revolution. Henryk Dulęba, a very close collaborator of Waryński, believed in 1878 that the revolution would begin 'in ten months'. Filipina Płaskowiecka announced that 'the revolution will begin in the Skierniewice region', while Dulęba placed it 'in Częstochowa'.¹ Waryński, more than some of his comrades, combined a romantic faith in the immediate coming of the millennium with the realistic judgment of what was possible. First, to get in touch with real proletarians, he found work as a locksmith in the largest metal factory in Warsaw, Lilpop & Rau. He became very popular among his workmates. A future friend of his, who described how he heard him for the first time, remarked that Waryński had 'the art of accommodating himself to the degree of intellectual development of his listener – to undergraduates Waryński spoke in the students' style, to the workers as a worker; both understood him perfectly... because his words were always the expression of deeply held convictions'.[2]

In the 'propaganda circles' members hotly discussed the ideas of Karl Marx, Ferdinand Lassalle and Mikhail Bakunin. At larger meetings, which sometimes attracted sixty participants and were, against all conspiratorial rules and simple commonsense, held in open spaces in the Warsaw suburbs, the talk was about less abstract matters and more about the daily worries of the workers.

Apart from general propaganda, Waryński initiated the formation of 'resistance funds' in factories. A participant who later became a leading member of the 'Proletariat' describes[3] how these fund-raising circles were soon transformed, mainly by Waryński, into socialist groups, which in June 1878 numbered some 300 members, a very large membership considering the times and the dangerous police conditions in which they had to conduct their underground activities.

At this time the influence among Polish socialists of the German Social Democrats, then the largest socialist party in the world, and closest to Marx and Engels, was evidently very considerable. The Warsaw socialists needed printed material to support the propaganda they spread by word of mouth among the students and the more literate workers.

We at once went to work. A few popular German pamphlets were translated. Some propaganda brochures were written and all manuscripts were in January 1878 taken by K. Hildt [one of the socialist intelligentsia] to Leipzig. The printing was finished in April 1878, but the most difficult task was left: the transportation of 6000 copies from Germany to Warsaw. Waryński undertook to accomplish it; it suited him as a man who was blessed with singular courage and rare sangfroid in the most dangerous situations. Without any knowledge of the German language, not having any connections in the frontier pass he went to Germany (illegally) and after a few weeks returned to Warsaw with parcels of books, which he carried single handed through the frontier.[4]

One can understand the feelings of the memoir-writer (who at the time he wrote had long before severed his links with this brand of Polish marxism and become a leading member of the patriotic Polish Socialist Party), who more than a quarter of a century later described thus the emotions of those days: 'The enthusiasm in the workers' and students' circles after his return cannot be described; we grasped the pamphlets, joyful as children, the first printed socialist word in Polish – Ludwik's name was on everybody's lips.'

We find very few details in the rare memoirs of the survivors of 1878 in Warsaw about the intellectual debates among the first Polish socialist groups. But in September 1878 they produced the results of their thoughts and debates which they called 'The Brussels Programme', and which was better known as the 'Programme of Polish Socialists' (Brussels was used as a means of deceiving the Tsarist gendarmerie who had been hunting this first Polish subversive movement since 1863).

From what we know it is clear that this small group of young men and women, who could only with difficulty lay their hands on smuggled marxist and revolutionary literature, seriously debated a whole range of economic, sociological and political problems which were, at least in their eyes, cognate to the situation of the Polish nation.

The first thing they analysed was the emergence of Polish capitalism (whose representatives were often non-Poles; in some of the later Polish marxist publications this fact was to be adversely commented on). Would it give birth to a liberal bourgeoisie, as was the case in France or England? or would the Polish entrepreneurs always loyally serve any power which would defend their property? Another question was the timing of the social revolution. Would it happen very soon? If this were to be the case, was there any sense in widening the battlefront to attack not only the possessors of economic power, but also the government? In other words, ought the Polish socialists to concentrate only on socialist propaganda and economic struggle or should they fight the Tsarist government as well? The next difficult problem was their attitude to patriotic, national tasks. Was Polish independence and the liquidation of the partitions a matter which should interest social revolutionaries? Would this not divert their energies to an aim which was not of pure class interest? Connected with this was the theoretical and practical question: should the Polish socialists in the Kingdom of Poland combine forces with Russian, Lithuanian and Ukrainian revolutionaries, who all lived in the same Tsarist state, or should they look to the Poles in Germany and Austro-Hungary as their natural comrades and co-fighters ? And the last great question was : by what means could they bring about the revolution ? Was propaganda, agitation among the masses, the organising of Resistance Funds and strikes enough ? Or should they, as the Russian revolutionaries were already doing, employ physical terror ? And if terror had to be used, should it be directed against the economic exploiters or against the political oppressors, or both ?

In time the Polish socialist movement, the orthodox marxists and the patriots, were to see the complexity of these problems in a more sophisticated light. But basically they were to remain the divisive intellectual and emotional forces which from the beginning rent Polish socialism.

The Programme of Polish Socialists, published in Warsaw in the autumn of 1878, was, as was to be expected, vague on some answers to these problems and confused on others. But its appearance was the most important step on the way to the creation, four years later, of the International Social Revolutionary Party 'Proletariat', with a more definite programme. We must therefore look more closely at its content.

Before we do so one cautionary remark is necessary. The most authoritative text of the Programme of Polish Socialists which has survived was published in the first issue of the Polish socialist periodical *Równość*, which first appeared in Geneva in October 1878. But we know now that this was an edited version of the Warsaw original. The socialist historian, Adam Próchnik, said firmly that a very important paragraph on national independence was omitted by the Geneva editors. He said :

It is characteristic that in this first programme of Polish Socialism in 1878 the aim of national freedom was included. The dispute about that [aim] among the historians of Polish socialism . . . was finally . . . resolved in a positive manner. The later [October 1879] emigré edition of the [Brussels] programme, in the endeavour completely to eliminate political aims, removed this point.[5]

On the other hand, another Polish historian, basing himself on

Russian sources, ascribed the more nationally conscious version
to a separate document which another group of Warsaw socialists
was supposed to have circulated in the same year, 1878.[6]

The Programme[7] opened with the statement:

In every society all social, economic and political institutions are the result of
the common, age-old endeavours of all members of society, without exception,
and ought therefore to serve everybody's benefit. But because of the fact that
an insignificant minority of society now possesses the means of production,
i.e. capital, only they reap the exclusive advantages of these institutions.

These relations between the capital-owning minority and the
propertyless majority made labour a market commodity. Following this Marxian definition of the economic relations existing in
industrial society between the capitalists and workers, came the
well-known conclusion that the price of labour was solely
dependent on one condition: the fluctuation between the supply
and demand of available labour in the market.

All other social and state institutions were dependent on the organisation of
hiring labour. The so called 'individual freedom', which was based on the
famous idea of 'self help', has been reduced to a struggle in which the victor is
the capitalist whose strength is material means. Deprived of the means of
production, deprived of the possibility of independent work and reduced to
the role of a hireling, the worker loses all moral independence and becomes
obedient to the will of capital in every manifestation of his individual and
social life.

The accumulation of economic and political power in the
hands of the possessor classes had evoked a reaction in the
toiling masses who, by adopting socialist theory, aimed at
making those powers serve the interests of society as a whole. To
achieve that aim there must come 'a radical change of existing
social relations...i.e. the social revolution'. The Programme then
touched on the Polish national problem:

We have come to the conclusion that the triumph of socialist principles is a
necessary condition for the successful future of the Polish nation, that active
participation in the struggle against the established social system is the duty
of every Pole who values the fate of millions of the Polish people above the
interests of the gentry-capitalist section of our nation.

The Programme then proceeded to enumerate the main aims
of its authors. These were divided into eight heads: the first

demanded that society should assure to every individual a 'many-sided development of his natural faculties'. The second aimed at transferring all the means of production from private hands to common ownership by the toiling masses and 'thus hired labour will change into collective labour in associations, in factories, workshops and farms'. The third point of the Programme stated that 'everyone has to share the benefits accruing from collective labour, a right which the toilers will scientifically determine in the future'. The fourth point called for 'complete social equality of all citizens irrespective of sex, race or nationality'. The fifth paragraph asserted that the realisation of these aims was the task of all working men, and therefore, 'the social revolutions must be universal and international'. The sixth point, which became the guiding light for three generations of Polish marxists, asserted the need for 'federal associations with socialists of all countries'. The seventh point expressed the belief that the 'implementation of these principles can be achieved only by the people under the moral leadership of a popular organisation, conscious of [the people's] rights and interests'. And the last point firmly asserted that 'the basis of our activities is the moral consonance of the means employed with the established goal'.

The next part of the Programme dealt with the main means 'for the development of our party'. These were: (*a*) 'organisation of popular forces'; (*b*) 'the propaganda of socialist principles by word of mouth and writings' and (*c*) 'through agitation, i.e. protests, demonstrations and in general through active struggle against the present social system, in the spirit of our principles'. This part of the Programme concluded that 'because of the ineffectiveness of legal means the Programme can be achieved only through social revolution'.

The last part of the Programme of Polish Socialists summarised the basic resolutions of the Geneva (1866) Congress of the International Workers' Association (the first Socialist International) and affirmed the Poles' loyalty to its principles, among which again the international and class character of the struggle for socialism was underlined and repeated again and again.

What strikes one in the Programme is its complete lack of any concrete demands, corresponding to the political situation then existing in the Kingdom of Poland and the economic conditions in which its industrialisation was taking place. Secondly, there is the complete ignorance of political power as an element which should play a part in the 'established social system', which they wanted to overthrow. The government in St Petersburg was not even mentioned; neither was Tsarism. And while there was talk of 'the fate of millions' of Poles, the question of their cultural, not to say national, freedom was never considered. As we shall see later, when the first Polish marxists had their own publications, in which they discussed their ideas more thoroughly and in greater detail, these omissions, especially on national problems, were to emerge as basic, and divisive, principles among Polish socialists.

The first Programme's formulations on 'associations of labour' and international 'federations' bore witness to the influence which Bakunist and Proudhonist ideas exerted on the early Polish socialists. But all the other formulations in the Programme were of unmistakable marxist origin. The materialistic explanation of historical development, the stressing of the monopolistic role of class, and of class struggle, in determining the social content of human evolution was patently of marxist origin.

The 'Programme of Polish Socialists' of 1878 laid the foundation of the first fully developed Polish marxist party, which was formally born four years later.

ARRESTS AND EMIGRATION

While the authors of the Programme ignored the government, the latter's political police did not overlook the manifestations of the subterranean activities of the Polish socialists – the first political conspirators in the Kingdom of Poland since the suppression of the 1863–4 insurrection.

The Tsarist authorities were vitally interested in keeping down the political temperature of Polish society as much as possible. The revolutionary Populist movement in Russia proper had already passed through the more peaceful phase and was turning more and more towards radical manifestations and even to direct personal acts of terrorism against the highest representatives of the established system. It was therefore important not to increase the tension in the empire. The ruler of the Kingdom of Poland, its Governor-General Kutsebou, was ready to tolerate more than was then lawfully permissible. Some years before the first Polish socialists started to clarify their ideas and organise their activities, there arose spontaneously solidarity self-help Funds, organised by workers in many Warsaw factories. 'The factory managements and the police looked at them through their fingers', remembered a participant in this movement.[8] No arrests were made among the members of the Funds, no pressure was used to disband the first organisations of Polish workers.

But Waryński and his friends, who at first tried to infiltrate the groups forming the Funds, so as to change them into socialist-action circles, soon came to the conclusion that most of its members were not interested in wider political ideas but only in direct self-help activities. The socialists decided therefore to form groups, known as Resistance Funds, which, as their name implies, were meant to serve as a financial buttress for strikers, or for those workers who might because of their militancy be thrown out of work. Soon this, too, was not enough. A new organisation known as the Revolutionary Circles appeared among Warsaw workers.

The number of members of each such Circle was limited to between ten and fifteen. Each Circle elected a treasurer and an organiser. The organisers in turn formed an Organisers' Circle, where matters of organisation were decided by a majority vote. Each of the organisers could be empowered to form special circles of members or non-members of the party, and even of those who did not agree at all with the party programme, but who were ready to help in special cases in organisational activities.[9]

According to the same source, the organisation formed special groups for Propaganda among youth; contacts with groups of Polish socialists in the Kingdom outside Warsaw and in the empire; finance; publications; smuggling across the frontier of socialist literature printed abroad, mainly in Germany but also in

Switzerland; propaganda among women and maintaining contact with arrested comrades and for helping their families.

This was too much for the secret police, especially as two members of the 'Revolutionary Circles', both workers (Karol Skowroński and August Michalski) decided, for pecuniary gain, to betray their colleagues. The organisation numbered then between 200 and 250 members.[10] For an underground organisation this was a large membership. For the Tsarist authorities who were inclined to let sleeping dogs lie in the Kingdom, these betrayals came at a moment when the red light started flickering. Arrests were ordered. They occurred in two large waves, in 1878 and 1879. Altogether 137 persons of both sexes were involved.

Count P. E. Kutsebou, the Governor-General, in a letter dated 8 September 1878[11] to the governor of Warsaw, General N. Medem, ascribed the appearance of socialist propaganda in the Kingdom to an influx of German workers – socialists who were forced to emigrate from their country to Poland as a result of Bismarck's repressive laws against the German Social Democratic Party. There certainly were German-speaking workers among the pioneers of socialism in Poland. Between 1882 and 1884 the Proletariat published some of its leaflets in German (especially for Łódź and the surrounding region). But the Germans did not play a leading or even an important role in the Polish socialist movement, then or later. On the contrary, some Polish socialists, especially of the orthodox marxist brand, in later years occupied a prominent place in the German Social Democratic Party, of whom the best known are Rosa Luxemburg, Julian Marchlewski, Karol Radek and Leon Yogiches-Tyszka. The Tsarist authorities had the choice of at least two methods of smothering the new sparks of rebellion in Poland. On the basis of a new law in 1878 they were able to hand over those accused of any criminal political activity to the military tribunals; but the prosecution had to prove actual rebellion or an assassination plot. Any political trial had to take place in the imperial capital, in open court, with speeches of advocates, who might, as they often did, use the proceedings to preach liberal ideas. The Tsarist government had at this time enough trouble suppressing its native *Narodniks*. On the other hand, the Kingdom of Poland had been singularly quiet for more than a decade. The Governor-General in Warsaw therefore accepted the opinion that 'the open court in such a case [as of the arrested Polish socialists] could become the spark, which may [again] inflame passions, which have already calmed down'.[12]

He therefore decided to punish the socialist culprits administratively. This could mean a small fine, or a few months' imprisonment in a fortress on Polish soil; or it could be merely a slight inconvenience by making the offender live for a time in a specified place and under the surveillance of the police. But the Tsarist authorities could also, without trial, exile an unwanted person to the most remote eastern regions of Siberia, and that for many years.

Unfortunately, events developed more dramatically and ended more tragically. One of the arrested socialists was the very impetuous 17-year-old apprentice, Józef Bejta. On 12 July 1879 he quarrelled with a young soldier, who was on guard in the prison of the Warsaw Citadel. Bejta not only refused to leave the window in his cell but started to throw at the soldier bits of the mesh covering the window. A shot was fired, killing young Bejta instantly. Another prisoner, Maria Hildt, called from her window to the other prisoners: 'break the windows and destroy everything'. A riot started. The prisoners used any weapon they could lay their hands on, breaking windows and destroying the furniture in their cells. The wardens and gendarmes had to fight a real battle. In thirty-six cells the windows were broken. At one moment, when the riot looked like being suppressed, Lieutenant-General Ulrych, the commandant of the Citadel, started visiting the cells personally to appeal to the prisoners to calm down, and also to explain the circumstances of Bejta's death. When he arrived in cell 34 its occupants, both students, 25-year-old Stanisław Landy and 19-year-old Wacław Sieroszewski (later a writer of some distinction), attacked him, one with a large piece of wood, and the other with a piece of his iron bed. The General was probably struck on the head, although he himself denied it at the later trial (it would have meant a certain death sentence for the attacker, but the Tsarist authorities were at that time against the creation of Polish martyrs). This physical assault could not be dealt with administratively. The Governor-General therefore ordered a military tribunal to try Landy, Sieroszewski and also Ivan Kleshtchevnikov, the private of the Kolivansky infantry regiment who had shot Bejta. The soldier was acquitted. Landy was sentenced to twelve years' hard labour in the ore mines and Sieroszewski to eight years in a fortress prison. Kutsebou decided to reduce the punishment for both by exiling them for life to remote regions in eastern Siberia.[13] The first chapter of the martyrology of Polish socialism thus began.

It is of interest to note the influx of workers into the pioneering groups of Polish socialists. Among the 137 arrested for belonging to socialist organisations in Warsaw in the years 1878–9, 79 were members of the intelligentsia, but even at that time 58 were workers.[14] A few years later, the proportion of intelligentsia to workers was reversed.

From the end of the eighteenth century, Poles in danger because of their political ideas and activities had emigrated. Traditionally, they used to go to France, to Britain or even to the new 'land of the free', the United States, where Tadeusz Kościuszko became a national hero.

This time most of the socialists chose a neighbouring country, Austria. The main reason was the hope that they might spread the new gospel of socialism as formulated in the Brussels Programme among the Poles in Galicia. But they were no doubt also attracted by the comparative freedom under the law which existed in the constitutionally governed Austro-Hungarian empire. Although very much under the influence of Tsarist conditions and Russian revolutionary thought, they knew from their own experience how great is the difference between a limitless autocracy, as Russia then was, and a régime such as Bismarck's Germany, which, however oppressive, was yet subject to constitutional law[15]. In July 1878 five leading Warsaw socialists, Ludwik Waryński, Kazimierz Dłuski, Stanisław Mendelson, Kazimierz Hildt and Jozef Uziembło, escaped to Galicia.

Some soon left for Geneva, to establish there a centre of socialist thought and publications, which for more than a decade played a very important role in the pioneering years of modern Polish socialism and marxism. Waryński went first to Lwów, where since the early seventies a periodical called *Praca (Labour)*, connected with the printers' trade union, had been disseminating vaguely socialist ideas. He left soon for Cracow, partly because the police were paying too much attention to him as a Russo-Polish revolutionary, and partly because his temperament was not such as to allow him to be easily accommodated in a movement which was more interested in an immediate amelioration of working-class conditions than in utopian and revolutionary ideas.

Cracow was then the centre of Polish culture. It had that rarified air of sophistication in which even the most abstract and politically unreal ideas can find enthusiastic followers. Waryński, as always a romantic, founded in Cracow a clandestine socialist organisation, modelled on the one which had just been smashed in Warsaw. Its members were mostly pupils of the Teachers' Seminar, the School of Arts and of the higher grades of the gymnasia, together with some workers. After a few months the police penetrated the organisation and arrested thirty-five of its members, who stood trial before the court in Cracow accused of spreading 'subversive socialist ideas' as a part of an 'international conspiracy'.[16]

The jury at the trial, which lasted from 16 February until 16 April 1880, acquitted all the accused of criminal intentions and activities. Waryński was the centre of the proceedings. He defended himself, and used the occasion of the open court, with all the legal privileges attached to it, to propagate his ideas of economic change and the new system of social relations that he envisaged.

Waryński stated that the so-called Brussels Programme (which, as we know, was written in Warsaw in 1878) represented his socialist ideas. He made, as a historian of this movement noticed,[17] the important point that Polish socialists considered it to be their task to prepare for a universal, as opposed to a national, social revolution. Therefore their comrades-in-arms could be Russians, Germans or any other revolutionaries, but not those Poles who did not pursue the same social and economic goals. The next important point he made was that the socialists of his persuasion considered economic change to be the only important and determining factor worth fighting for. Political and social changes would be the automatic result of the economic transformation of existing society. According to Waryński, socialists ought to recognise the scientifically discovered laws of social development, and concentrate on destroying or radically changing the economic basis of capitalist society (he stressed at the Cracow trial rather the latter definition, perhaps because of his role as a defendant). In the best Marxian vein he then announced that the political superstructure would collapse like Samson's temple.

The Cracow jury consisted of respectable members of the Polish middle classes, who certainly heartily disliked the cosmopolitan and even anti-patriotic views of Waryński and his co-accused. But they rejected the case of the state prosecutor and found guilty of only minor offences some of the accused who, like Waryński, lived under false names. Those of them who were Russian subjects, like Waryński and Uziembło, were expelled from Austria. They went west, to Switzerland, where the earlier Polish socialist emigrés had already laid the foundation of organised activity.

In Geneva, a group of socialist emigrés from the Kingdom of Poland, mainly those who had escaped arrest in Warsaw in the late seventies, came to the conclusion that for the time being it was for those who lived abroad to keep alive the ideas of the young Polish socialist movement. They started a periodical in which Polish socialists could express their views. They also hoped to smuggle it into all the three parts into which Poland had been partitioned, and thus in time rebuild their shattered organisation. In October 1878, therefore, there appeared in Geneva the first socialist periodical in the Polish language, *Równość* (*Equality*). Its first editors were Kazimierz Długski, Witold Piekarski and Szymon Dikstein. After their virtual acquittal at the Cracow trial, the editorial board was enlarged by including Ludwik Waryński and Stanisław Mendelson. Both soon became the most influential members of the board. Mendelson, who was the son of a Polish–Jewish banker, and his wife, Maria, who came from a rich Polish

Roman Catholic land-owning family in the Ukraine, were the financial backers of the enterprise. What was intended to be only a temporary expedient, an outpost to deal with emergencies, became a permanent institution, which lasted for at least 25 years. The Geneva socialists acknowledged the so-called Brussels Programme, as their ideological credo. The first issue of *Równość* opened with the publication of this Programme. Most of the articles in that issue, as in later ones, were commentaries on the Programme, or polemical articles against those who criticised or disagreed with it.

The paper included in every issue articles describing the situation in Poland, and also lengthy notes about the socialist and labour movements in other countries, mainly in Russia, Germany and Austria. And while the editors admired the revolutionary terrorist actions in Russia, at the same time they noted positively the achievement of the growing peaceful labour movements in Britain, Germany and Switzerland.

As is usual with every political emigration, the Polish socialists in Geneva, theorising hundreds of miles from Warsaw, Łódź and Białystok, were inclined to 'clarify' their ideas. What this meant was a sharpening of the logical conclusions of the more vague formulations arrived at at home. One of their first problems was to define their attitude to the question of Polish independence; of a national state; and of the preservation of Polish culture and its institutions.

It is fashionable in present-day People's Poland to present the early Polish socialists as orthodox marxists who, at least theoretically, laid the groundwork of the Polish communist movement in our century.[18] They certainly rejected Karl Marx's and Friedrich Engels's strongly and consistently held views of the need to restore a Polish independent state. In 1875 Marx wrote:[19]

There is no contradiction in the fact that the international workers' party [meaning the First International] aims at the resurrection of the Polish nation. On the contrary – only then, when Poland regains her independence; only when as an independent nation she is again able to conduct her own affairs, only then will it be possible to start again her internal development, only then will she be in a position to co-operate in the social transformation of Europe.

Friedrich Engels, who, like his close friend Marx, took a very lively interest in Polish affairs in general, and particularly in the development of the Polish socialist movement (he wrote a special introduction to the 1892 Polish translation of the Communist Manifesto), had a very poor opinion of the stand taken by the *Równość* group on the Polish national question. He made this clear in a letter he wrote on 7 February 1882 to the German socialist writer Karl Kautsky, in which he said:[20]

History yet proves that a great nation, as long as it lacks national independence, has no conditions even for a serious debate about any of its internal affairs ...The international proletarian movement is possible only among independent nations ... As long as Poland is partitioned and vanquished, there can be no development of socialist parties inside the country, no German proletarian parties will be able to establish real international links with any Poles other than those Poles who are emigrés. Every Polish peasant and worker who awakes from his stupor and starts taking part in matters of general concern meets the fact of national subjugation as the first obstacle in his path. The removal of this obstacle is a basic condition of any healthy and free development. Those Polish socialists who do not put the liberation of their country at the top of their programme make me think of German socialists who do not demand before everything else the repeal of the [Bismarck] laws against socialists, the introduction of freedom of the press, association, and the right to hold assemblies. To be able to fight one must feel the ground under one's feet, and air, light and space. Otherwise everything else remains empty talk.

It was the irony of Marx's influence in Poland, that his most fanatical followers in other matters utterly rejected his views on the future of their country as an independent state, and consequently refused to have anything in common with those Polish socialists who, like him and Engels, considered a liberated and united Poland to be the precondition for the establishment of socialism. Until 1942 the term 'social patriot' was used by Polish marxists to denote those who fell from socialist grace by caring for the nation.

In its issue of November 1881 *Równość*[21] published an article under the title 'On the role of the Polish owning classes'. It appeared unsigned and was in fact a declaration by the editorial board on the most important questions which confronted the early Polish socialists. It rejected vehemently the idea of fighting for special Polish national interests. It stated firstly that *Równość* faithfully adhered to the main slogan of the Programme, 'Social and international revolution'. It then went on to say:

we, to be truthful, do not believe in any national ideas or in a special 'national spirit' . . . we do not believe in all that because (1) We are not engaged in nursing 'the national spirit'. (2) We are materialists and we comprehend the history of our nation, as of other nations to be outside the sphere of all kinds of 'spirits' and 'missions'. History, in our understanding, was and is the struggle of two classes, of two social elements hostile to each other: beginning with lords and slaves, patricians and proletarians, then a feudal class and its subjects, and reaching the end of its evolution in the struggle of the capitalist against the proletarian. It will come to a certain culminating stage, when the class struggle will be solved, but then there will be no more resurrectors [meaning those who aimed at resurrecting an independent Poland].

The article then accused the patriots of cynicism for 'by talking about the common interests of Polish lord and peasant, of factory owner and worker it gives you the chance systematically to fool the people'. And to make their position as clear as possible they said, further, 'there exists an economic law which rules the present economic system and competition. This [law] transfers capital and labour from country to country, and does not know state frontiers or nationalities. Capital and competition denationalise everybody and everything.'

The phrasing of this statement may not have been very sophisticated. The flaw in its logic is easy to detect. Its historical assertions are certainly untrue. Its perspectives have shown themselves to be erroneous. But it is a valid popularisation of the main ideas of the Communist Manifesto. It was the spiritual guide for two or three generations of Polish marxists. It is therefore a document of more than historical interest.

Because of this rigid anti-patriotic stand of the marxists in *Równość*, some of its members broke away from the organisation. The most prominent of them was Bolesław Limanowski, who, with a few of his political friends, formed a separate Polish socialist group called 'Lud Polski' (The Polish People). In its programme, which was published in August 1881 and was called 'The manifesto of the socialist association "Polish People"',[22] the group round Limanowski stated that the gentry had finally lost the right to lead the Polish nation. The new bourgeoisie born out of 'the magnates, the affluent urban middle class; the alien elements who are voracious exploiters' had betrayed the nation's interests. Only 'the people' (meaning the peasants), the artisans, the small shopkeepers and the new class of industrial workers were now the 'basis of existence' and hope of the nation. The 'Polish People' socialists opted for common ownership of the means of production ('land, factories, and tools') and for production co-operatives. At the same time they put high on their list of aims the 'ending of political and national oppression by the [creation of an] independent national life within voluntarily accepted frontiers'. These last three words were used to skirt the problem of where the frontiers of the future Poland should run. Marx and the First International proclaimed the right of a future independent Poland to return to the frontiers of 1772, i.e. where they were before the first partition. In practice this would have meant the incorporation of many millions of peoples of Ukrainian, Lithuanian and Byelorussian background. 'Polish People' were, as one can see, more flexible in this matter.

What they rejected was the rigid class outlook of the Polish marxists and their cosmopolitan, or a-national, attitude to the question of the future of their divided nation. For quite a time they were merely a small group of emigrés. They had no organised followers in the Kingdom, where most Poles lived. But in less than fifteen years they were to become the dominant influence in the Polish socialist movement which in effect lasted until December 1948, when the organised remnants of the Polish Socialist Party were involuntarily merged with the communists to form the Polish United Workers' Party.

The majority of the *Równość* group decisively rejected any notion of a struggle for purely national interests. They made their standpoint very clear at a public manifestation which they called in Geneva on 29 November 1880, ostensibly to commemorate the fifteenth anniversary of the 1830 insurrection, but in reality 'to tell their comrades, the European socialists, what are the aims of the Polish proletariat, what are its goals and intentions'. According to a contemporary report[23] more than five hundred persons, consisting of Swiss, German, French, Italian, Russian and, of course, Polish socialists and revolutionaries, attended the meeting. In the chair was the prominent German veteran socialist and friend of Marx, J. F. Becker. Secretary of the meeting was Vera Zasulich, then a leading member of the Populist 'Tschorny Peredyel', who was to become later one of the first Russian marxists in her friend Plekhanov's Liberation of Labour group.

Four members of the former general council of the International Workers' Association (First International), Karl Marx, Friedrich Engels, Paul Lafargue and F. Lessner, were unable to travel from London to the Polish meeting in Geneva but sent a long letter of support. This was for them not an empty formality. In their letter Marx and his friends highly praised the democratic and later socialist revolutionary character of the modern Polish national movement. Starting from Kościuszko at the end of the eighteenth century, they remembered the prominent Polish historian Joachim Lelewel, who with a group of Poles publicly supported the Communist Manifesto in 1848, underlined the part played by Poles in creating the First International and paid homage to the many Polish revolutionaries who fought and died defending the Paris Commune in 1871. They opted for the patriotic socialists. As they said,

the cry: 'Long live Poland', which was then [in 1830] heard all over western Europe was not only a tribute of sympathy and admiration to patriotic fighters, who were vanquished by brutal force. With this call a nation was greeted whose uprisings, for her so fatal, always stopped the counter-revolution's march; a nation whose best sons never quitted the defensive war, fighting everywhere under the flag of the people's revolution ... Hence outside their country's borders the Poles played a great role in the struggle for the liberation of the proletariat – they were everywhere her front fighters.

And the letter ended, 'Today, when this struggle is growing among the Polish people, they must be supported by propaganda, by the revolutionary press, and be linked with the striving of our Russian brothers; this will be one more reason for repeating the former cry: "Long live Poland".'

Ludwik Waryński spoke at the meeting in the name of the Polish socialists. He was already their acknowledged leader, at home and in temporary emigration. His ideas had become more mature, his aims more precise. The Polish proletarian revolution, he declared, will be no further chapter of the futile national uprisings. Its goals will be those of the International. The Polish workers and socialists will fight their last battle together with their close allies, the Russian revolutionaries. He therefore spoke in Russian, and addressed himself directly to the Russian comrades in the audience.

From the first sentence of his speech Waryński persistently stressed the deep gulf which divided Polish socialists from any other class or political movement in Polish society. This was certainly a full-blooded marxian interpretation of social life. The only names he mentioned in his speech, Alexander Herzen and Mikhail Bakunin, who supported Polish freedom fighters, were both Russian revolutionaries. According to Lev Deich,[24] who was very close to Waryński in his Geneva period, the latter was a declared marxist ('Waryński and Dikstein on innumerable occasions, at meetings and in private talks, declared themselves marxists. Both many times publicly disputed things with Zhukovsky and Kropotkin, who were, as is known, enthusiastic supporters of Bakunin'). But evidently Waryński had no warm feelings for Marx, with whom he never established any personal contact.

At the beginning of his speech Waryński said: 'We appear before you not as fighters of a future Polish state to confront you, [as] the subjugated subjects of the Russian state; but as representatives and defenders of the Polish proletariat, and you as the representatives of the Russian proletarian cause.' He then proceeded to explain why neither during the Polish uprising of 1830 nor at the time of the insurrection of 1863 did their leaders co-ordinate their endeavours with the Decembrists or latter-day Russian revolutionaries. And his answer to this question was sharp and plain:

the differences which divided the Polish secret organisations from the Russians, and made co-operation impossible, became clear. The Polish gentry wanted not a revolution but respect for its ancient privileges. Loyalty, the fear of revolution, detestation of any social reforms, that was what was demonstrated by the leaders of the insurrection. All their endeavour was directed towards the murdering of the movement...The Polish revolutionaries were afraid that the movement in Russia might go further than anticipated, that there might possibly occur a repetition of the Great French Revolution with the revolting Dantons and Marats. If it should ever come to common action – thought the Poles – then it will be only on the condition that we assure for ourselves full separation and independence in settling all home matters.

Never before had a Polish political leader condemned in such uncompromising terms so many painful but heroic chapters of his nation's history. But Waryński was, until his premature death in a cell in the Schlisselburg fortress nine years later, a man who did not know the meaning of the word compromise. His language was not that of an objective historian, but of a passionate partisan. He did not stop at condemning the leaders of the Polish rebellions. He rejected the very idea of national struggle. He quoted an anonymous speaker at a meeting called to express solidarity with the 1863 uprising: 'Poland', said this speaker, 'suffers, but there is a nation which suffers much more than Poland – they are the proletarians all the world over. We ought to think about their liberation.' Waryński then criticised the leaders of the International who 'have not used their influence to subordinate the Polish cause to the universal programme of proletarian emancipation'. And he bitterly complained that 'even the creators of the Communist Manifesto link their immortal slogan: "Workers of the world unite" with another which may attract the bourgeoisie and the privileged classes in general, the slogan: "Long live Poland!"' He darkly suggested that by showing 'admiration and sympathy for the Poland...of exploiters and exploited' they persisted in keeping alive 'former political speculations'. He probably had in mind Marx's belief that the German revolution would come about only after Tsarist Russia had been forced back to the frontiers it had prior to the first Polish partition in 1772.

He then ridiculed the conception that 'Poland has to defend the West against Russian despotism'. Vera Zasulich, the person taking notes at this meeting had, as he said, fired 'the first shot proclaiming the new battle, which started in Russia... * This

---

* Vera Zasulich in 1878 shot and wounded Trepov, the Governor of St Petersburg.

shot announced to Europe the coming emancipation – the fall of the giant.' Here he discerned the only guarantee of liberation. In the Russians he recognised the comrades-in-arms of the revolutionary Polish socialists. And he ended his declaratory speech, the political programme for his generation of Polish marxists and for many who came after him:

We are not the fighters of 63 who are all inflamed by a hatred of Tsardom and who perished on the national battlefields. We do not represent states hostile to each other. We are natives, members of one big nation more unhappy than Poland, the nation of proletarians. The standard of this nation is our standard, its interests are our interests, its victory will be our victory.

When he made this speech Waryński had only three more years of life in freedom. He ended his political existence when he made his last speech as defendant before the war tribunal held in Warsaw between 23 November and 20 December 1885 which sent him to die in a solitary prison cell. During the few remaining years of his life he changed some of his opinions. As we shall see, he moved away from the utopian dream of a social revolution which would solve old problems, an idea which he inherited mostly from the Russian Populist revolutionaries; and later became convinced that the way to win the workers over to socialist ideas was to combine revolutionary goals with demands for reforms of the conditions in which they then lived. But Waryński never modified his hostility towards patriotism, towards any activity in a national cause, with non-proletarian, non-revolutionary democrats. When the subjugation of the Poles was mentioned in any document which the early Polish marxists published, it was usually followed by an assurance that only in common with other oppressed, Russians or Germans, would the Poles achieve their liberation.

The Polish marxists, then still known as the *Równość* Group,* used the socialist congress organised by German Social Democrats, but with the participation of other nationals, which took place in the beginning of October 1881 in Chur, Switzerland, to

* Although in August 1881 *Równość* ceased to exist because of a quarrel among its Board members, they soon came together again as members of the new periodical *Przedświt* (*Dawn*).

gain support for their anti-patriotic stand against the small Limanowski group, and against Marx. After a heated debate in which Waryński played the main part, the congress adopted a resolution proposed by the French socialist, Benoît Malon, which pointedly said: 'The congress, considering that the struggle for emancipation is a struggle of classes, and not of nationalities, dismisses the questions raised by the Polish [Limanowski Group] delegates.'

Stanisław Mendelson, one of Waryński's close collaborators, whose father's money made possible the publication of the monthly *Równość*, and from 1881 *Przedświt*, established good relations with German Social Democrats who had been living in Switzerland since the promulgation of Bismarck's anti-socialist laws. He and his wife were specially close to the Social-Democratic member of the Reichstag, Georg V. Vollmar, with whom they were corresponding.*

But the closest personal and ideological contacts of the Polish emigré marxists were with Russian socialists who then still belonged to the *Narodniki* movement. These were the small 'Tschorny Peredyel' group, whose most important members were Georgy Plekhanov, Vera Zasulich and Paul Axelrod. They were already shedding populist ideology for orthodox marxism. According to Lev Deich, Waryński, Dikstein and other Poles established during their stay in Geneva very close personal contacts with the Russians. For a time they practically lived together in a sort of commune in a nearby village. Waryński often spoke at Russian meetings and 'made a deep impression' on his listeners. 'Thanks to him we Russians not only had a good understanding of the general character of [socialist] activities in Poland, but were also initiated into its debates; we knew about particular occurrences.' And although when it came to co-ordinating policies, the Polish marxists of this period unhesitatingly chose the influential terrorists of the 'Narodnaya Volya' although these were nearer to Bakunin than to Marx, Deich can be believed when he remarked that the close relations of 'Waryński and

* This correspondence is now with the Internationaal Instituut voor Sociale Geschiedenis, Amsterdam.

Dikstein with our group, to which Plekhanov then already belonged, had also some influence on them.'[25]

From the long talks and debates between the Poles and the Russians came the idea of preparing a programme which should elucidate the Poles' stand on their relations with Russian revolutionaries, and also prepare the way for united action against the régime. Again, the Russians took a direct part in preparing the letter 'To Russian socialist comrades', which was dated 'Geneva, 3rd November 1881', and signed by a 'group of former members of *Równość* and the editorial board of the socialist periodical *Przedświt*'. 'We, the "tchernoperedyeltsy", says Deich, 'completely agreed with their [the Poles'] initiative, and thereafter discussed point by point the outline of their appeal to the Russian comrades. The draft was improved and enlarged, especially by Plekhanov; it was accepted by everyone.'[26] After the 'Appeal' was first published in Polish in numbers 7 and 8 November 1881 of *Przedświt*, Deich translated it into Russian.

The appeal to the 'Russian socialist comrades'[27] consisted of three main parts. The first dealt with the conditions in which the revolutionary struggle was taking place in Tsarist Russia. After acknowledging the fact that in western Europe the socialists and 'radicals' had their task of organising the 'cosmopolitan struggle' against the bourgeoisie made easier because of the existence of 'some freedoms', the Poles considered the lack of any freedom in Russia to be a decisive hindrance to achieving the 'economic emancipation' of the working classes. They acknowledged the prime role of the 'Russian comrades', who had taken upon themselves the whole burden of terrorist activities. The Poles declared their full solidarity with 'Narodnaya Volya'. In the second part of the Letter they discussed at length the 'so-called national Polish problem'. The Polish socialists-marxists developed their anti-nationalist ideas with great clarity and sincerity; this was to be the characteristic mark of one of the trends of the Polish Labour movement for years to come.

They made it clear from the beginning that the 'so-called Polish national problem' was in fact the question of an independent Poland. This they rejected as a possible objective of revolutionary struggle. 'At present', they wrote in their 'Letter to the Russian comrades', 'the social, economic and historical evolution of Polish society deprives this problem of its former vitality; what is left of it among some groups of urban population...is consciously used as a weapon against socialism by our enemies: the conservative gentry and our anti-radical bourgeoisie.' As far as the peasantry, 'which on average makes up 70 per cent of the whole population in all three parts of Poland' was concerned, the authors asserted that

the peasant masses, with very insignificant and rare exceptions, have always acted in a hostile manner against the uprisings for the national independence of Poland...Today because of the fact that the land was given to them by the partitioning powers, and not by Poland's privileged classes, the peasants have become even stronger opponents of nationalism, linking their notion of nationalist movements with the hostility they felt for their economic exploiters. The only way to move this numerous mass of the Polish people is in the name of economic demands.

And therefore, said the Poles,

for us, socialists, the national problem has basically nothing in common with socialism; and because it is based in practice on the unity and solidarity of classes, it can for us be only of negative value, as a hindrance to the development of socialist consciousness among the working classes and as a harmful factor in the cause of freedom in general.

The authors then stated their conviction that 'as everywhere else, socialism for us is an economic problem which has nothing to do with the national question, and expresses itself in real life as a class struggle'. To achieve socialism one must develop socialist consciousness among the workers 'on the basis of their class interests', and one must fight for political freedom in Russia.

And here came the most important part of the 'Letter'. The Poles, believing, 'as the discussions with the Russian comrades last year' had shown, that the character of a socialist-revolutionary organisation was 'exclusively influenced by general economic interests and political conditions', declared themselves against any socialist organisation built on the basis of 'ethnographic national frontiers'. In other words they rejected the idea of a party which embraced Polish socialists from all three partitioned parts of the country. 'A Socialist Party of Poland cannot exist as one entity; there can only be Polish socialist groups in Austria, Germany and Russia, which together with the socialist organisations of other nationalities form in the given state an organisational union; this does not preclude them from uniting among themselves as with other socialist organisations.'

The last part of this sentence must be understood as a concession to the sympathisers of the patriotic-socialist group round Limanowski. It is vague in the extreme, and was no doubt meant to be so. The Poles then proposed to the Russians to form 'one universal socialist party, which would consist of the socialist organisations of different nationalities in the Russian state'; that the 'organisations which fight independently in the sphere of economics and politics ought to amalgamate to act unitedly'; and that there existed 'the necessity to work out a common political programme for all socialists who are active in the Russian state'.

Repeating again the proposal to work out a common programme, the Poles assured the Russians that although 'you will be accused of Muscovite centralism, and we will be branded as traitors to the national tradition' by patriotic Poles, 'these accusations will have no influence on our common endeavours' because 'for us the time of separation and traditional animosity has passed away'.

The Polish appeal to the Russian revolutionaries and socialists was sent to both wings of the now divided Populists: to the terrorist 'Narodnaya Volya' and to the group calling themselves 'Tschorny Peredyel', some of whom were very soon to become the adherents of marxist social-democracy. The former, who were at the time of much greater importance and influence, were then paying dearly for the successful terrorist action against Alexander II (in March 1881). The second group consisted mainly of the intelligentsia. Neither of the two Russian groups formally answered the Polish appeal. They were apparently too busy with their own affairs, too harassed by the Tsar's gendarmerie to take up the Poles' suggestions of a common programme for a new, all-Russian revolutionary party.

But for the Poles their Letter to the Russian comrades was a

most important document. It expressed the views of the great
majority of Polish marxists for many years to come.

Some of the Poles who escaped to the West after the arrests of
1878–9 in Warsaw and the Cracow trial, and who published first
Równość and then *Przedświt*, acquiesced in their role of political
emigrés who were able to use their intellectual energy only as
writers and debaters. Waryński was first and foremost a man of
action, an agitator, an organiser, although he was also intellectually
one of the most able of the first generation of Polish marxist-
socialists. His married life was also not very successful and he
found the life of an emigré unbearable.

The Russian group of which Plekhanov was the leading spirit
collected the money[28] which made it possible for Waryński to
return, illegally of course, to Warsaw. In December 1881, under a
false name, he crossed the German–Russian frontier to find
himself again in the Kingdom of Poland. In the coming months
his name was to become indissolubly linked with a momentous
act in the history of the Polish socialist movement.

4 A PARTY OF MARXIST REVOLUTIONARIES

THE FORMATION OF THE SOCIAL REVOLUTIONARY PARTY 'PROLETARIAT'

When Waryński arrived in Warsaw, the negative effects of the police repressions of socialist groups were slowly beginning to diminish. Even in the summer of 1881 some of the active members of the clandestine socialist 'circles' had started to come out of prison. The most prominent among them were Kazimierz Puchewicz and Henryk Dulęba. Both their families belonged to the gentry. Puchewicz was able to graduate at the University and to join the ranks of the intelligentsia. A man of systematic thinking, devoid of the deeper emotions and passions, he accepted in marxism the apparent logic of its economic reasoning. He considered, at least at that time, both political goals and the struggle to achieve them to be a waste of revolutionary energy. For a time he helped in the formation of the party. Dulęba was unable, for lack of means, to finish his secondary education. He became a locksmith in the repair workshop of the Vistula Railway Line. Because of his lively intelligence, personal courage and great tenacity as an agitator, he played a prominent role in the first mass organisation of Polish workers who had accepted socialist ideas. For a time, and this was the most decisive period in the pioneering stage of the first Polish socialist party, these two and Waryński constituted the formative core of the new movement.

It was mainly through Dulęba that old contacts with sympathisers in factories, which had been broken in 1878–9, were slowly re-established in the winter and spring of 1882. Soon, socialist groups reappeared in the largest Warsaw factories of Lilpop, Handtke, Orthwein, and Schulze, in the railway workshops, and in the factories of Ostrowski and Karski. Not only

51

workers but also artisans and apprentices were brought into the new movement. These latter groups, which consisted of the better-educated members of the newly emerging Polish working classes, played an especially prominent role in the formation of the party.

The other important element in the revived movement was the students of the Warsaw University, who were often joined by Poles who were studying in St Petersburg, Moscow, Kiev, Odessa, and Wilno. Those of them who thought of more than a personal career found the materialistic 'Warsaw Positivists' a poor substitute for the idealism which had inspired their fathers and grandfathers in a life of struggle and noble sacrifice. Socialism, first in its populist-anarchistic form, and later in the respectable marxist clothes of a scientifically proved philosophical and economic system, attracted many of the educated young Poles. And because it was a forbidden idea in the Tsar's Russia and its disseminators became the martyred prophets of a new faith, the dry, rational theories of Marx glowed with a romantic light, which responded to a deep emotional need in many of the best young men and women in this part of Europe. If the word 'proletariat' meant the social underdog, they put themselves into this category without great intellectual difficulty even if they were descended from the gentry or affluent Jewish bourgeoisie.* As Poles or Jews, they were all underdogs in the Russian empire. They were a constant opposition who needed a theory. After the catastrophe of 1863 pure Polish nationalism had not yet been rehabilitated. The idea of a revolution, which must first totally destroy and then completely rebuild, had not yet been compromised. They accepted marxism as a rational theory and the revolution as a romantic idea.

A group of graduates of Warsaw and other Universities in Russia, among whom the most prominent were Stanisław Krusiński, Ludwik Krzywicki, Mieczysław Brzezinski, and

---

* Stefan Zeromski and Stanislaw Brzozowski have described the evolution of a significant part of the young Polish intelligentsia who in disgust with their elders' 'betrayal' of idealism chose socialism and marxism as their new creed.

Zygmunt Heryng, translated Karl Marx's *Das Kapital* (it appeared in Polish in 1886 in Leipzig and succeeded in passing the Russian censorship to be freely sold in Warsaw bookshops).[1]

The Western socialist influences which reached the Poles through the writings of Karl Marx, Friedrich Engels and Ferdinand Lassalle were continually supplemented by the practical examples of revolutionary activity that occurred in the East. Young Poles born in what are now the Ukraine, Byelorussia, and Lithuania, or in the Baltic provinces, were especially susceptible to the tragic heroism of 'Narodnaya Volya'. In 1880 or 1881 Wincenty Rutkiewicz formed a Polish group of the Russian 'Narodnaya Volya' in Warsaw University, of which the leading members were Józef Wojnilowicz and Henryk Jackiewicz, both born in Vitebsk, Franciszek Rojecki and Jan Slizien from Podolye, and three members of old Polish–Jewish families: Leon Winawer, Feliks Kon and Wacław Handelsman. They were among the many who assimilated the background of the Russian revolutionary populists, and who brought its traditions and political practices into the first Polish marxist party.

After Warsaw it was St Petersburg's Polish students who contributed most, numerically, to the formation of the Polish party. In 1881 the Polish group in St Petersburg had a membership of twenty-five extremely able young men and women. Some of them later became leaders of the party. The most prominent were Stanisław Kunicki, born in Georgia of a Polish father and a Georgian mother, and Tadeusz Rechniewski, whose father, although a member of the Polish gentry, became the vice-President of Libau on the Baltic. Many of the St Petersburg Poles were also members of 'Narodnaya Volya', as also were the members of the Polish socialist groups in the University towns of Moscow, Kiev and Wilno (where Poles, Jews and Russians, intelligentsia and workers, worked together).

It was characteristic of the close ties which bound the early Polish socialists to the Russian revolutionaries that Waryński's first contact with native Polish marxists at the beginning of 1882 took place in the house of a Russian civil servant in Warsaw.

E

Mikhail Dobrovolsky, a 45-year-old justice of the peace, a sympathiser with the Populists, whose close personal friend was the Polish socialist Maria Izbicka, made his home a meeting place for the marxist group which undertook to translate *Das Kapital* into Polish. Soon he himself was deeply involved in the debates of the Polish marxists about the prospect of change in the Kingdom of Poland. The debates were heated because one of these marxists, the highly intelligent Krusiński, believed in the automatic political and social consequences of capitalist development in the Kingdom. He considered that Waryński's ideas of forming a party which would hasten the process of change was dangerous for its participants, and historically unnecessary. He was one of those marxists who were ready to leave the future to history's automatic processes.

But it was Ludwik Waryński who won the confidence of the working-class groups and students 'circles', for whom the reading of marxist tracts was not enough. Although 'Narodnaya Volya', after the assassination of Tsar Alexander II, was being destroyed by police action, its terrorist successes were too fresh in everybody's memories to lose its attraction for the most oppressed subjects in the empire. The Polish newspapers widely, and in general objectively, reprinted the political, economic and social gains of the growing trade unions and socialist parties in Western Europe. Naturally this strengthened the hands of those, like Waryński, who were eager for action.

For all practical purposes the framework of a party was already in existence. It needed an external impetus to formalise its existence, and make itself known to the public at large. A strike of two thousand workers in Warsaw performed this historical function.

The men employed in the workshops of the Warsaw–Vienna Railway Line had for some time been bitterly complaining about the behaviour of their chief foreman, a certain Altdorfer, who was forcing the workers to accept lower wages, and was, in their opinion, cheating them of the Pension Fund, to which they themselves had contributed. On 1 April 1882 a member of a smiths' delegation slapped the foreman's face during a violent quarrel with him. Gendarmes were called by the management, but had to withdraw because of the obvious excitement of the workers. Later, two of the smiths were accused of public violence. This only heightened the bitter feelings. On 3 April all the workshops downed tools. Two thousand workers assembled in the yard, demanding the immediate dismissal of two foremen whom they considered most obnoxious, and the reinstatement of the two smiths who had been sacked. The workers were surrounded by police and gendarmes, but showed no sign of being intimidated. The management had to promise fulfilment of all the demands of the strikers, who then returned to work. The victory was short-lived. As a contemporary observer reported,[2] 'The promises were naturally not fulfilled, the Railway agreed only to changes in the Fund's rules [concerning retirement pensions].'

It took the socialist organisation a full three months to find a printing shop which would agree, illegally, to produce a long, unsigned leaflet, in which the employees of the Railway's workshops were called upon to organise resistance against the persistent wrong-doings of the management and its 'lackeys', the foreman and some of the 'loyal' workers. The leaflet called on the Railway employees, in connection with the approaching election to the board of the Pension Fund, to choose colleagues who were determined to defend the workers' interests. The leaflet contained a significant passage about the way to deal with 'traitors' among the workers. It recommended: 'With spies and those who do us wrong, let's deal quietly, without witnesses or anything which could leave a trace, then not we but they will become afraid of us.'[3] This was the first step on the road to personal, although limited, terrorism, which in the end cost the party more than it did those against whom it was directed. The influence of 'Narodnaya Volya' is here direct and obvious. And although the Russian revolutionary movement was already paying dearly for having adopted physical terror as its main political weapon in the struggle against Tsarist autocracy, the Polish socialists included it in their political arsenal. It must here also be noticed that the call for the use of terrorism was connected not so much with its deployment as a universal political tool, but as an instrument to be deployed in defence against traitors and police spies. One must always remember that the young Polish working class was of peasant stock. And in villages, far from courts and other institutions which meted out justice on the basis of legal processes, it was the tradition to settle especially obnoxious moral crimes, among which the betrayal of confidence took the first place, by direct and personal punishment. The authors of the post-strike leaflet were thus talking in a language which could be easily understood by its readers, accepted by them as a traditional reaction against immoral people, and which gave satisfaction to people who otherwise felt weak and helpless.

The leaflet to the workers in the Railway's workshop opened a new chapter in the history of the Polish Labour movement. More than a year later, in September 1883, in a leading article in the first issue of the clandestine periodical *Proletariat*, Ludwik Waryński described this period[4] as

living a life separate from that of the toiling masses, even with the best intentions they [socialists who came from the 'bourgeois-gentry intelligentsia'] have the greatest difficulties, in coming close to their daily needs, to the living reality. They always occupy the lofty ideal heights, they defend the idea's purity and integrity against the shabby daily struggle, they become abstract figures, missionaries forgetting that only during the gradual mass struggle does the idea change from word into flesh. Our movement also passed through this phase which was initiated by the young intelligentsia. It was always based on propaganda, on the enlightening of the working class about the final consequences of the present system and the role of the masses in historical evolution, but it never got embroiled in the daily life, in the often sometimes stubborn daily struggle against capital, and never reached the point of agitation. But experience, coming from the closer contact with the world of labour, has brought the conviction that the socialist movement, if it is not to remain without influence on the masses, has to pay great attention to daily life, has to live with it, and not with theory, has to take part in the smallest even manifestations of working class life, always taking its position on the side of the toilers, defending their rights and interests – in a word, propaganda has always to move hand in hand with agitation and the struggle against the burden of oppression. Our present work is built on this basis...
Experience has persuaded us that a decentralisation of the movement, the full independence of groups and individuals and their federal unity would lead only to disorganisation, to anarchy, making public the ways and means of action and opening for the enemy a real possibility of introducing his followers and spies into the organisation. The centralist organisation of our enemy leaves us only one efficient weapon in the fight against him: the centralisation of the revolutionary forces and the surrounding of ourselves

with the greatest secrecy which only becomes possible when applying the former [centralisation].

The criticism of the intelligentsia in this article was directed against men like the group who were busy translating Marx's *Das Kapital*, and even more so against Kazimierz Puchewicz, whose Warsaw group of students and workers survived the mass arrests of the late seventies, and who was a strong adherent of the Western, and especially, German Social Democratic Labour movement; he was against any terrorist activities, any premature political action, until the socialist groups could educate and organise a large part of the Polish working classes.

In the summer of 1882 Waryński, who was in favour of immediate political action, and of formalising the existence of the party which would inspire and lead it, received formidable support for his policy. The fiery Stanisław Kunicki arrived from St Petersburg, where he had been studying in the Institute of Road Engineering. He had the mandate of the Polish socialist students in St Petersburg and he was also personally connected with the leadership of the terrorist 'Narodnaya Volya'. Kunicki was an impatient young man, inclined to what we would now call political adventurism. His mixed Polish–Georgian background made him easily receptive to romantic ideas about the role of the will in politics. He met Waryński, and became fascinated by the man. Two years later, during the investigation after his arrest, he said of Waryński:[5] 'This man at once draws you to him, he was the first who presented the problem in such a way that I agreed with him wholeheartedly. His programme became mine.'

The meetings of the group which was discussing 'the problem', as Kunicki called it, of forming a party and giving it a programme, consisted for two months of three persons: Waryński, Puchewicz and Kunicki. By the beginning of August everything was settled. The party was to be called: Social Revolutionary Party 'Proletariat'. Later the word 'International' was sometimes prefixed to its name. ('Social' in Polish is interchangeable with 'socialist'.) On 15 August 1882 the programme of the new party appeared in Warsaw, produced on a hectograph. Fifteen days later on 1 September 1882, the programme, this time printed, of course illegally, began to be distributed in factories and in the University. The first Polish socialist-marxist party had been born. Its life was short. Only four years later most of its leaders and active members went either to the gallows or were sent to the farthest corners of Siberia, whence only a few returned alive. But its influence on the political evolution of the nation became a lasting element in its modern history.

'PROLETARIAT': ITS PROGRAMME AND ORGANISATION

The platform of the first Polish socialist party was published as a pamphlet under the title 'Manifesto of the Workers' Committee' of the Social Revolutionary Party 'Proletariat'.[6] It is divided into six parts. In the first part, the authors explain the source of 'misery and every kind of oppression in society' as the consequence of the 'unjust division of resources...among the classes'. This occurs because the 'privileged classes...do not work productively, [but] seize the overwhelming part of the wealth created through labour. The working class, robbed of the fruits of their endeavour, has to endure misery and degradation.' The Programme then proceeded to show that this class-division in society was not a recent phenomenon, but had existed 'for ages'. All former social systems were built on exploitation of the propertyless class by the privileged. Only lately had the class-conscious proletariat started a 'mass struggle demanding complete economic, political and moral liberation'.

The second part of the Programme was devoted to the evolution of contemporary Polish society. Its authors stated that 'our country is no exception: the past and present of its systems, based on exploitation and oppression, gives our workers nothing but poverty and disgrace'. The existing system was described as: 'bourgeois-capitalist', which has an 'ailing appearance' because of 'lack of political freedoms'. The Programme complained that in face of the degrading conditions of life (misery of the masses, prostitution, etc.) neither the exploited nor the privileged few had shown any sign of 'personal dignity'. 'Gold and lust – they are the only aims in the lives of our possessing classes; misery, oppression and ignorance – they are the essence of the life of a Polish worker.'

This humiliating situation of the Polish working class was not alone the result of the existing political circumstances ('the dependence of our country on the invaders'); it was no less the consequence of the 'national movements and insurrections' which by calling for national unity were 'killing in our society the class consciousness of...the working class'. Therefore any modern popular movement in Poland must first and foremost 'free itself...from the hostile class interests of the privileged classes, governments, and national traditions'.

The third chapter of the Programme of 'Proletariat' began with the assertion that 'the interests of the exploited cannot be reconciled with the interests of the exploiters' and declared categorically that 'the Polish proletariat completely severs its link with the privileged classes, and rises against them as an independent class, quite different in its economic, political and moral aims'. The Programme then affirmed its belief in the common fate of workers of different countries and solemnly declared that 'the Polish proletariat...is one...with all exploited no matter of which nationality'.

The fourth chapter formulated the goals of the party. They were divided into three parts: the first dealt with economic aims, the second with political problems, and the third was, characteristically, dedicated to improving the 'moral life of the Polish proletariat'. As in former cases where the definition 'moral' was used by the early Polish socialists, it included both ethical and social problems. The economic part of the Programme, 'in accordance with the socialist principles, adopted at international congresses by the proletariat of all countries', demanded that:

(1) the land and the means of production should pass from individuals to become the common good of the workers, the property of the socialist state; (2) that hired labour should change into collective labour, organised in factory, artisan and agrarian associations; (3) that every individual should have the right to benefit from the fruits of collective labour, in proportion to the amount of work offered and the general resources of the state.

There were two, slightly different, published versions of the political aims as formulated in the Programme. In the first version, which appeared only in hectographic form with the date of 15 August, and which was not included in the printed edition which appeared a fortnight later, there was talk of a possible independent Poland, but not for the time being, as a practical proposition.[7] What appeared in both versions of the Programme was the demand for 'the greatest amount of freedom' and the threat that 'we will fight against every government irrespective of its nationality until we have achieved all these freedoms'. And further: 'We condemn unreservedly the lack of freedom of conscience, language, assembly, associations, speech and in print.' The concrete demands were:

(1) The self government of political groups [in all probability they meant autonomy for the different nations inside Russia]; (2) everybody's participation in law-making; (3) election of civil servants; (4) full freedom of speech, press, assemblies, associations, etc., etc.; (5) full equality for women; (6) full equality of religions and nationalities; (7) international solidarity as the guarantee of universal freedom.

What was conspicuously lacking in the political part of the Programme was an alternative to the existing political régime in Tsarist Russia. On one hand, the party opted for all kinds of freedoms usually connected with the achievements of the liberal West. But there was not a word about the way these freedoms might be achieved, safeguarded and developed. Parliamentary democracy, an independent judiciary or any other institution elected by popular vote, whose functions should be the checking of the power and activities of the executive, were never even mentioned. The problem of having a government sympathetic to the aims of the party was not even discussed. There are those among the historians of the 'Proletariat' who explain these extraordinary gaps in the party's Programme as one more proof that the 'Proletariat' considered the Russian 'Narodnaya Volya' to be the headquarters of political revolution in the empire and whose responsibility was the formulation of the political aims of the all-Russian revolution. The Letter of 1881 to the Russian Socialist Comrades gives support to this assumption. A document produced by 'Proletariat' in February 1884 openly proclaimed the dominant position of the Russian revolutionary organisation as leader of the political struggle against Tsardom (we shall return to this document later). Yet it must still surprise anyone familiar with Polish history that the Polish socialists entirely discarded the traditions of native radicalism, which since the end of the eighteenth century had striven to achieve parliamentary democracy. Indeed those who formulated the first programme of a Polish socialist-marxist party tried hard to break with all traditions of the gentry's past, and not only with the bad ones. The anti-democratic tradition in Polish marxism is older than Lenin's Bolshevism.

Then came what the Programme called 'moral' demands. Some were straightforward social aims, such as that 'education should be obligatory, free of charge and undenominational', or 'religious affairs should be independent of the State'. Next came moral desiderata which could with much greater effect have adorned any man's wall, such as: 'The relation between sexes should be based only on sentiments', or 'work should be considered a duty and an honour'. The authors then went on to declare, this time in the best marxist tradition, that 'the emancipation of the working class from the economic, political and moral yoke must be achieved by the workers themselves'. This was the *raison d'être* of the formation of the social-revolutionary organisation 'Proletariat', of which the Workers Committee had taken on the leadership of 'the economic and organisational struggle'. The Programme then stressed that as the distinct interests of the 'Proletariat' 'as the exploited class' emerged most glaringly in the sphere of economics, 'we will in our struggle have foremost in mind especially economic relations'. Taking into account political conditions then existing in Russia, 'we are forced to work and act in secrecy, emerging only with mass actions in proper moments'.

The fifth chapter of the Programme dealt with the means which the party would use to achieve its aims. And, as before, this chapter was also divided into action in the economic field, politics and 'morality'.

In the economic struggle the party intended to: (1) 'incite the

workers against all forms of exploitation; (2) organise com-
binations [strikes] and secret workers associations; (3) terrorise
capitalists and their servants for their inhuman treatment of the
workers or for calling on the police during the workers' conflicts; (4) to found, as far as possible, associations consisting of
workers only.'

The political weapons 'in the struggle against despotism'
must help the party to 'weaken and disorganise the Tsarist
government'. Therefore the party's activities would aim:

(1) By our resistance to thwart the administration's actions; (2) to incite the
population against paying taxes; (3) resist government orders which are
directed against the workers; (4) stubbornly to oppose any interference on
the part of government organs in the conflicts between workers and factory
owners; (5) openly to manifest our sympathy with all those who fight against
the despotic Russian government, considering them to be comrades-in-arms;
(6) to participate in anti-government demonstration; and, lastly, (7) we will
punish spies, traitors and in general all those who because of personal
advantage betray the cause.

The means of 'moral improvement' were listed as: (1) 'the removal of prejudices' spread by 'the clergy, the press and the false
guardians'; (2) the lifting of the moral standards of the workers
and the reawakening of their human dignity; (3) the production of
literature, 'which will let the people find out the scientific truth,
free from the subversive tendencies of the exploiters'. The authors
stated rather solemnly that in their activities 'we will hold fast to
the principle that only that which is scientifically proved, which
defends the right things and speaks in the name of truth' could
be helpful in the moral development of the proletariat.

The final chapter, the sixth, consisted of three sentences only.
Its essence was that the emancipation of the workers could be
achieved only in unity, in one centralised organisation led by the
Workers' Committee. It would work clandestinely only as long as
conditions forced it to do so. And they called on 'all workers in
the cities and villages' to participate in their activities.

The stress the authors of the party's Programme laid on
'terrorising capitalists and their servants' who behaved in an
exceptionally inhuman way towards their employees, and the calls
to 'punish spies, traitors' and others who 'betray the cause' were

sentiments very widespread in all sectors and among different trends of the contemporary revolutionary movement. In the middle eighties the father of Russian marxism, Georgy Plekhanov, wrote with approval of the Russian revolutionaries, who, as he said, 'will not withdraw from so-called terrorist activities, if this should seem necessary in the interest of the struggle'.[8] But, as in the case of the Russian Populists, the use of physical violence by the Polish marxists, although very limited in its theoretical scope and rarely practised, acted as a boomerang. It evoked a violent reaction from the government authorities. In the end, the physically and numerically weaker party paid the costly price of defeat by a more brutal opponent. The Tsarist gallows and Siberian mines not only brought death to its leaders but also liquidated the party itself in the space of three or four years.

But to the enthusiastic young pioneers of the first Polish marxist party the possible dangers were seen in the romantic light of a new dawn. They believed that the Social Revolution was imminent and would come either from the East, in Russia proper, or from the West, the seat of the half-mythological International, which was then already immobilised by the quarrel between the followers of Marx and Bakunin, but which the Poles still saw as an immense force for world revolution.

It is true that an organisation called 'Proletariat's Red Cross' was formed as one of the branches of the party, to which non-members were also recruited. It was the task of this organisation to look after comrades who might be caught by the police and imprisoned, and to help their families, after the bread-winners had disappeared. In time, this by-product of the party organisation played a decisive role when the final curtain was falling on 'Proletariat'. For the time being the party's Red Cross was extremely useful in giving those among its sympathisers, who were either not willing to accept the full party obligations or were not considered by the leadership to be the right material for membership, a role to play in its support. Until the summer of 1883 the police knew little or nothing of the existence of 'Proletariat', and even if some of its members were arrested, they were released, at the most to suffer the slight inconvenience of reporting from time to time to the police. The Red Cross collected funds, which could be also used for not strictly samaritan work.

The most important task of the new party was to build and develop its organisation. It had, of course, to work underground. Socialism, even of the mildest kind, was outlawed in the Russia of the Tsars as soon as it tried to apply itself to existing political and social conditions. But it was not only a socialist party that was prohibited even from being born; any association of workers created to defend their interests as employees was considered to be subversive, and was therefore banned. Thus 'Proletariat' was able to adopt the social theories of Marx or Proudhon from the West, but its organisation and activities had to be based on the conspiratorial experience and example of Bakunin and 'Narodnaya Volya' in the East.

In the archives of the Tsarist police there survived the only written copy of the statute (prepared in 1882) of the 'Workers' Committee', which initially (until the spring of 1883) was the name of the high command of the party.[9]

The statute consisted of fourteen paragraphs. The first described the Workers' Committee as the body which 'organises propaganda among workers'. The second paragraph laid down that the Workers' Committee should form 'Workers' Circles', and establish a network between the leadership and the rank and file. From other reports consisting of statements made by members of 'Proletariat' who were subsequently arrested and who confessed under interrogation,[10] we know that such 'circles' consisted of five or six, but never of more than ten members, of whom the most knowledgeable and reliable became the leader, known as 'organiser'. The members of the circle attended 'meetings' and 'encounters'. At the former, propaganda speeches were delivered, often by the leader, Ludwik Waryński, himself. The target was always the capitalist class, and the iniquity of the system of exploitation that it created. The speeches usually ended with a call for organisation and for a show of militancy in the workshops. Sometimes the members asked questions to which the speakers from the Workers' Committee replied. Often the meeting was devoted to the reading of clandestine political literature (some of the members of 'Proletariat' were illiterate), and its distribution for further circulation among their friends. Every member of a 'circle' was also obliged to pay a weekly contribution of 5 kopeks to the party's funds, for which he was given a formal receipt the following week, stamped by the Workers' Committee of 'Proletariat'. The 'encounters' were only for those members of the 'circles' who had to perform a special task and who had to be given instructions by the leadership, or who were given larger amounts of clandestine pamphlets or leaflets for distribution. The members of the circles were, as a rule, unknown to each other, and their names were known only to the 'organiser', a wise precaution against police spies and agents-provocateurs. The meetings of the workers' circles generally took place in public houses and restaurants, where a room would be hired, supposedly for a modest meal. 'Encounters', too, were held in such public eating places, but also in parks, squares or on street corners. The 'Workers' Circles' were due to meet once a week at a prearranged time and place. The delegates of each 'circle', who formed a 'section', also met once a week.

The Statute in its fourth paragraph described the purpose of the leadership as being to 'agitate on the basis of the daily interests of the workers and thus not to miss anything, which demonstrates the present-day misery of the workers'. The authors of the Statute had evidently no great hopes of being able to use the methods of socialist parties and trade unions to the west of Poland in improving the lot of their own proletariat. The next paragraph was the only one in the whole Statute that dealt with action, other than agitation and propaganda. It laid down the rules for using terrorism. Paragraph 5 stated: 'Recognising that in some cases terror is the only weapon against the political rulers, the capitalists, spies, etc. the Workers' Committee forms a social [fighting] organisation.' And further: 'After each act of terror the Workers' Committee will publish a statement'. The next paragraph laid down that all decisions of the Workers' Committee 'are arrived at by a majority vote.'

The Workers' Committee,* according to Statute, was the only body entitled to co-opt or expel its own members. And again we are told that 'the task of the Workers' Circle is to organise a militia, which will defend the party members against state spies'.

The last four paragraphs of the Statute discussed interesting details of the party organisation. We are told that the Workers' Committee 'has its agents, who are divided into two categories'. Then came the vital detail: 'the duties of the agents of the first category are unlimited and are the same as those of the members of the Workers' Committee; they take the place of members who have left'. And at the very end: 'at meetings [of the rank and file], members of the Workers' Circle appear as agents'. This was probably considered good camouflage to keep secret the actual membership of the leading party body. Nothing is said about the procedure for forming the central leadership. The Committee just emerged, and developed by co-option.

The formal announcement of the founding of the party, the publication of the Programme, and the lively interest this evoked among radical students at Warsaw and other Universities in Russia, even the hostile reaction in some newspapers in the Kingdom and in Galicia, together with the boldness of the small group of leaders, found a quick response in the factories and workshops. Whatever we may now think about the proletarian mystique in marxism, its religious belief in the exceptional historical mission of the workers to abolish themselves as a class by liquidating all other classes, there can be no doubt at all that when the working class was economically defenceless, inferior socially and only the object of political power, marxist dialectics, otherwise incomprehensible, became as real a force as divine law had formerly been. The belief that by scientific methods the secret of humanity's history had been decoded, and that the weak and the meek of today's society were destined to become its rulers tomorrow, or in the next few years (the first Polish marxists

* After the Wilno conference, of 1883 the national leadership adopted the name 'Central Committee', leaving the term 'Workers' Committee' to be used by local organisations.

were, like all millennial fanatics, certain that the all-liberating Social Revolution was a question at the most of a few years), was the origin of the incredible psychological transformation which occurred among the most wretched actors in the Polish industrial revolution. Torn up by their roots from the roadless, isolated villages, lost in the formless workers' city suburbs, subdued by the soulless actions of the machines, enslaved as cogs in the powerful wheel of a system which had no function for them other than to demand their physical labour, those of them whom the 'Proletariat' propaganda had touched suddenly discovered themselves as part of something forceful, members of the vanguard of historical change, builders of a future society. As long as this new brotherhood seemed invincible, strong in their bonds of secret and almost apocalyptic hope, challenging emperors and magnates, the members of this new movement could look the past heroes of their nation proudly in the face. They were as brave and as courageous as the best, the most famous of them. Of course, when the moment of truth arrived, when the enemy crushed them physically, some of them collapsed. But the best never shuddered even in sight of the gallows, and never regretted the sacrifice of young lives.

The leaders of the new party were as enthusiastic as most of their followers, probably even more so. The secret party organisation, the clandestine 'circles', the hushed debates behind locked doors in modest little restaurants and *knajpas* were no longer enough. They had passed the point of enlightening 'propaganda', they expected 'agitation', direct contact between the believers in the creed and the mass of workers whose destiny it was consciously to make history from now on, to transform themselves from passive sufferers into tomorrow's vanquishers of their oppressors.

THE PARTY IN ACTION

Four months after the Social Revolutionary Party 'Proletariat' was announced, when the marxist analysis of Polish society in the

Programme of 1 September 1882 was just beginning to penetrate the 'circles' of workers and young intelligentsia who considered themselves socialists, the party leadership, the Workers' Committee, issued, on the very eve of the New Year,[11] its first call to action. It appealed to the workers to form in factories and railway workshops 'associations for the collective...defence of their rights and interests'. The party made it very clear that these workers' associations should function separately 'in each factory (or workshop), exploited by a capitalist'. The party thought of itself as the national organisation which would instruct and direct the separate local workers' groups. ('The Workers' Committee will watch over all such associations, will provide them with all necessary means and will resolve all their possible doubts.') The workers were called on to begin forming at once ('soon after the New Year') defence associations, whose most important task would be: 'to lead in a proper way every collective action or strike in the factory', to collect dues, 'to watch that the management of the factory or workshop does not harm the workers, and to resist any abuse', to 'assist the wronged and their families', and again, 'to punish spies and traitors who for personal advantage are sacrificing the interests of their comrades and of the whole labour movement'.

Soon more concrete action was mounted by 'Proletariat'. On 10 February 1883 (29 January old style) the *Warsaw Police Gazette* (No. 22) published on its first page an order by the Warsaw Chief of Police, General Nicolas Baturlin, which shocked the workers. In it he directed his subordinates to arrange a fortnightly medical inspection of all women workers employed in factories and other enterprises. The order was based on a decree issued in July 1864 but which had never actually been implemented until then. It was a practice known to professional prostitutes. Only three days later, on 13 February, the Workers' Committee was distributing a short leaflet[12] in which the planned indignity was described as an 'insult, such as the world has not witnessed'. And further: 'it is then enough to make a living out of work, to carry the stigma of a prostitute.' The Committee addressed itself to the men-workers: 'You have been slapped in the face, they want to degrade you – to try out your patience and submissiveness! How will you answer that? Will you allow the vile agents to torture the weaker half of your working class?' And the leaflet ended with the rousing call: 'Workers! Do not allow it to happen! Do not withdraw before the danger which threatens your class! Fight back the assault, even if this protest has to be paid for in blood. Death is better than shame!' And at the very end: 'They want a fight – they will get it!'

The party did this time speak in a language which everyone understood. It appealed to the most cherished Polish sentiment: honour. The leaflet, although naturally illegal, was printed in some thousands of copies and was widely distributed among factory workers. A few hundred were, during the long winter nights, plastered on the walls of houses. The members of the new party were full of enthusiasm and two daring well-to-do members of 'Proletariat' dressed themselves in smart winter coats and went distributing the leaflet in the Warsaw trams. They also went to the gates of some factories, gallantly kissed the hands of the home-going women workers and handed them the leaflet.

The mass of Warsaw workers were outraged. They had on their side the sympathy of all classes of society. The authorities, for the first time since 1863, faced the possibility of a physical clash between the police and the populace. They decided to withdraw. Ten days after the appearance of the 'Proletariat' leaflet the acting Governor-General, Baron Kruedener, after obtaining approval for his action from Count Dimitry Tolstoy, the Minister of the Interior of the Imperial Government in St Petersburg, declared the order of the Warsaw Chief of Police to be null and void. The party triumphed. On 9 March the Workers' Committee published a second leaflet, this time to women workers,[13] which registered the victory: 'The Government has withdrawn before the formidable posture of the indignant workers; it cannot and will not execute its order. You have thus won the first case in which you were supported by the mass of workers!' The leaflet then went on to stress the class substance of the struggle and called on the women workers to organise themselves in 'fighting associations', to raise funds to be able to help

F

'the persecuted women-comrades' and thus in future 'collectively to leave the workshops and to force the "lords" to retreat'.

The triumph of Waryński, Kunicki and their followers in the party leadership was not won without cost. Kazimierz Puche-wicz, the third most important member of the group which formed the 'Proletariat' and was one of the authors of its Pro-gramme, was from the beginning wary of the militant influence which the Russian 'Narodnaya Volya' exercised on some of the party leaders who came to Warsaw from Russian universities. He considered the tone of the party leaflets to be dangerously adventurous. He saw the young Polish working class as immature in thought, and organisationally too weak to take on both their direct employers and the whole might of the police and army. He therefore advised that for some time the party's actions should be limited to the field of industrial relations. Puchewicz was very much impressed by the Fabian tactics of social democratic parties in the West, who after the defeat of the Paris Commune in 1871 were very careful not to engage themselves in revolution-ary actions against their governments. He reasoned that to provoke the Russian imperial government in the Kingdom would result in the annihilation of the young socialist movement. When his arguments fell on deaf ears he broke away from the 'Proletariat', taking with him a small group of members, and the underground printing shop of the party. But in less than six months, police action, and the inability of his more evolutionary strategy to show results brought about the liquidation of his group, which called itself 'Solidarność' ('Solidarity'). They published one short leaflet, in which they outlined their views. They advised only actions which would immediately improve the economic situation of the workers. The modern communist historians of this period describe them as the first 'opportunists' in the Polish labour movement[14] and 'Solidarity' certainly foresaw the catastrophic fate of 'Proletariat'. They should, however, with more justice be remembered as the forerunners of those Polish social democrats who in later years built the mass base of a Polish labour movement. Their sin, if such it was, was to appear before their time.

The Tsarist authorities did everything possible to make young people impatient. They blocked all channels of peaceful protest and opposition. This became even more evident after Alexander III initiated his repressive policies in the aftermath of the assassination of his father in March 1881. In the Kingdom of Poland it meant first and foremost the suppression of anything connected with Polish culture and language. The forcible russification of the ten million Poles as envisaged by Konstantin Pobedonostsev, procurator of the Holy Synod and a close adviser of the Tsar, was implemented in the Kingdom by Alexander Apukhtin, the Chief School Inspector of Warsaw. He was a man of limited intelligence who hated the Poles. The students of the Institute of Farming and Forests in Puławy were the first to suffer under his harsh régime, when socialist books, among them the forbidden biographies of the Populist heroes Andrey Zhelyabov, and Sophia Perovskaya, were found in their library. Many were arrested and sent to the severe prison in the Warsaw Citadel. Apukhtin himself went to the Institute, and got a stormy reception from the outraged colleagues of the arrested students. He then suspended 129 students, of whom 57 were forbidden to join any university in the empire. This brutal act of a hated 'tchinovnik' started a solidarity movement among the students of Warsaw University.[15] Those who planned action against Apukhtin, the symbol of oppression of the Poles, also included a group of Russian undergraduates, members and sympathisers of 'Narodnaya Volya', who were studying in Warsaw. One of them, Evgeny Zhukovitch, found an excuse to be interviewed by Apukhtin, and then struck him in the face. He was at once arrested. A protest meeting was held by Warsaw students and was dispersed by police and the military. The Workers' Committee of 'Proletariat' joined the students, of whom some were members of the party. Having just lost its underground printing shop to Puchewicz's 'Solidarity', it was only able to stick written posters on the city's walls calling on 'everybody' to attend a public meeting in front of the university on 18 April at 10 o'clock in the morning. For the first time in twenty years large numbers of Poles assembled in the streets to protest against a political action on the part of the St Petersburg government. These mass meetings which were always dispersed by the police, with military units in the background, were repeated in the next two days. One hundred and ninty-nine students were suspended from the University for periods ranging between one and three years. The members of 'Proletariat' were among the most severely punished. Eight students, who were suspected of socialist connections, were sent to prison in St Petersburg. Zhukovitch was sentenced to 18 months in prison. The 'Apukhtin plot' (*Shodka*) was the first anti-government Polish mass movement since the 1863 uprising. It became the fore-runner of the famous school strike in 1905 in Poland.

While the action in the universities against Apukhtin appealed mostly to the educated classes in Polish society, the strike con-flict in Żyrardów left the deepest impression on the workers.

Żyrardów, a small town to the south-east of Warsaw, became in the second half of the nineteenth century one of the centres of the textile industry. In the early eighties the proprietors of the large complex of workshops, known as the Zakłady Żyrardowskie, were Hielle and Dittrich, Austrian Germans who never spoke a word of Polish. They employed some eight thousand workers, for whom they built houses, and for whose children they provided schools, a clinic and a nursery, and a fund for invalids. Compared with most other employers of that time they were by no means the worst.

At the beginning of 1883 the whole of Europe experienced an economic crisis which in Żyrardów at once resulted in the factory management cutting the wages of the workers. The first to suffer the cuts were the women. They worked fourteen hours, six days a week. The highest man's wage was 40 kopeks, but the women earned only 20–5 kopeks. The announced cuts meant a loss of 5 kopeks daily, and left the workers with only a starvation wage. As the wage cuts were announced some time before their implementation, the workers had enough time to consider how to resist them. On 23 April the women struck. The directors then called on the police to deal with the 'rebels', and they arrived in some force the next day. But persuasion from such a source had not much influence. On 25 April some men workers joined the women. The Warsaw governor, General Medem, then sent four companies of infantry and a 'polsotnia' (half a hundred) of Cossacks, who started to arrest the so-called ring-leaders of the strikers. This caused an explosion.

On the same day General Medem arrived in Żyrardów in person and appealed to the strikers to return to work. They refused, protesting bitterly against the system of fines existing in the factory, which they considered to be a means of cutting their real wages whenever the management wished to do so. Instead of returning to work the mass of the workers marched to the local prison demanding the release of their arrested colleagues. The soldiers panicked. A young officer gave the order to fire. Three workers, of whom the eldest was 19 (the two others being only 15 and 17), were killed on the spot or died later in hospital. Many more were wounded and a few soldiers were injured by stones. Although General Medem brought in more soldiers during the night, the situation got out of hand. The next day many departments of the factory were sacked and the homes of the directors attacked. Some of the mob also attacked Jewish shop-keepers in the town. The management and the authorities decided to appease the workers. In a written statement, personally distributed by the director, they promised that the working time would be shortened by an hour each day, that the women would receive their former wages, that special shops would sell goods at cut prices to the employed, that the wounded would be paid their wages and that they would be employed to the end of their life, that the strikers would be paid full wages and nobody would be victimised, that the most hated director (a certain Frank) would be dismissed, and that 'the fallen will get a magnificent funeral'.[16] The promises were kept in their entirety. Thousands of people, among them the factory directors and their families, walked all the way to the cemetery behind the cortège. Those arrested were freed. It was the first great fight and great victory of workers in Poland.

There is nothing to prove that the 'Proletariat' directly contributed to the organisation or leadership of the Żyrardów strikers. What is known is that the party's manifesto and leaflets published in February and March reached the Żyrardów workers on the eve of the strike and of the disturbances. The police alleged that Teodor Łąkowski, the strike's main leader, was a socialist.[17] It is an undoubted fact that the Żyrardów workers set an example to their colleagues in other industrial centres. Soon afterwards a strike, organised by a prominent member of 'Proletariat', broke out in the metal factory in Warsaw owned by Lilpop, after the workers' demand for higher wages had been rejected by the management. The strike had its stormy moments and the police were brought in to intervene, but in the end the workers won, although the leader (Ptaszyński) and a few of the most active strikers were sacked some months later. The party was still maintaining its conviction that without 'economic terror', directed against the factory owners and their plenipotentiaries, no strike action could be successful. The growing economic crisis, with the accompanying rise of unemployment, and consequent weakening of the market value of hired labour, only strengthened such convictions. What the leaders of 'Proletariat' failed to understand was the simple truth that by wanting to change the balance of power of an economically weakened and precariously organised working class with the help of physical terror they only evoked a much more powerful response from a mighty antagonist: the state authority. With all their pretence of having found in marxism a scientific method of understanding history and mastering the present, they succumbed to the romantic Polish tradition of 'high aims call up strength'. And, like earlier generations of their people, they paid for it with everything they had.

WORLD REVOLUTION OR NATION?

When in August 1882 the leaders of Warsaw's socialist 'circles' announced the formation of the Social Revolutionary Party 'Proletariat', they were conscious that they must open the new organisation to other socialist groups also, especially in St

Petersburg, Moscow, Kiev and Wilno, which had long been established. It was therefore decided to call together the representatives of these groups as quickly as possible, and collectively to debate the aims of a united Polish socialist movement, as well as the forms it should take.

After some preparation, never easy in illegal conditions, the delegates assembled in January 1883 in Wilno. It was a very small gathering. At the most there were nine persons present, but more probably only eight. Four were from Warsaw – Ludwik Waryński, Stanisław Krusiński, Alexander Dębski and Edmund Płoski; two from St Petersburg – Tadeusz Rechniewski and Stanisław Kunicki; Ludwik Janowicz came from Moscow and Leonard Rymkiewicz (the organiser of the conference) from Wilno. Another possible attender was Zofia Dziankowska, representing Kiev.[18]

The Wilno conference had to solve three main problems. On its decisions depended the very existence of the 'Proletariat', which was then only five months old.

The first question was: were the conditions ripe to end the period of educating socialists (this was known by the generic term: propaganda) and begin the phase of mass activity (that is, agitation)? Stanisław Krusiński, a brilliant theoretician, was a strong defender of the first opinion. He saw the young Polish working class as intellectually and emotionally quite immature and therefore not yet ready for any direct political or economic action. He advised that more work should be done among the mostly illiterate workers, to make them understand the elementary laws ruling society and determining their situation. All the other participants at the conference refused to follow this line of reasoning, which they saw as an excuse for political passivity.* Some were just enthusiastic optimists. Others believed, rightly, that practical experience in organised struggle was at least as important in educating the workers about their miserable existence as any lecture. Waryński and his closest collaborators in

---

* S. Krusiński soon afterwards withdrew from any active work and devoted himself to translating *Das Kapital* and writing articles on socialism for legal Warsaw periodicals.

Warsaw, who had learned much from their contact with real Warsaw workers, hoped to combine active organisation and struggle with socialist education. The practically unanimous decision of the conference in this matter signified assent for the formation of 'Proletariat'.

The second major question was the scope of the political activities of the party. The Wilno conference was torn between two trends: on the one hand it was strongly influenced by the ideology of 'Narodnaya Volya', with which most of the delegates were closely connected (especially Kunicki and Rechniewski who then, by all accounts, considered themselves more as members of 'Narodnaya Volya' than of 'Proletariat'), which concentrated all its energy on destroying, physically, the political centre of the system. On the other hand, their marxist background moved some of them to overestimate the political results, which they believed to be automatic and immediate, of economic action against the owners of capital and of the means of production. The conference chose a middle way. They unanimously approved of terrorism against the government and, as in the Letter to the Russian Comrades of 1881, they considered 'Narodnaya Volya' the only body capable of organising its execution. On the other hand, they stated that the government was a collection of bureaucrats, independent of and above the existing classes (this was also the point of view of many contemporary Russian revolutionaries) and should therefore be attacked only if it interfered with the aspirations and actions of the revolutionaries. They opposed the tendency of the terrorist groups to dominate the revolutionary movement. ('The conspiratorial centralisation should in no case aim at...too great a strengthening of its activities at the cost of socialist propaganda and socialist activities.')[19]

But the most important question which was in the mind of every participant at the conference was: should one socialist revolutionary party be created for the whole of Russia, to which 'Proletariat' would in time be affiliated, or, as the St Petersburg representative suggested, should the conference lay the basis of a Polish-Lithuanian-Byelorussian party (which would correspond with the pre-partition frontiers of the former Polish state)? Or again, ought 'Proletariat' to consider itself an independent party of Polish socialists and attempt to spread its influence and organisation to the other two parts (German and Austrian) of partitioned Poland? Here were the questions on the answers to which, as we know now, depended the unity of the Polish socialist movement until November 1918, the moment when a new independent Polish state again appeared on the political map of the world.

'Narodnaya Volya', after the course of political assassinations which culminated on 13 March 1881 with the murder of Tsar Alexander II, went through a deep political and organisational crisis, from which it never recovered. One of the participants in the Wilno conference, Stanisław Kunicki, was then at the very top of what was left of the Russian revolutionary leadership. The Polish socialists thus knew the perilous state in which their Russian comrades found themselves. Yet the Poles unanimously rejected any answer other than the first one; they decided on one all-Russian party with one programme and one centralised political leadership. By taking this decision they also determined the inevitable split in the Polish socialist movement, which was, until 1919, never really concerned with the problems of revolutionary as opposed to reformist socialism, but always, and to the very end of its independent existence, fought its internal battles round the question of what position a united Polish nation and its working class should take in its theoretical and practical activities.

In consequence of its decision about the future united all-Russian party the conference concluded that the organisation of 'Proletariat' should correspond to the structure of 'Narodnaya Volya'. This meant separate organisations for the workers and intelligentsia, each having its own leadership subordinate to the party's national leadership.[20] It should be added that, because of the state of 'Narodnaya Volya' at the time of the Wilno conference, its delegates cautiously decided that for the time being 'Proletariat' ought to establish only federal links with the Russians, leaving complete unity to the better future when the 'centralisation' would naturally have gained in strength.

The conference ended by appointing a central leadership, to

be known as the Central Committee of the party, consisting of seven persons: Ludwik Waryński, Tadeusz Rechniewski, Stanisław Kunicki, Alexander Dębski, Edmund Płoski, Henryk Dulęba and Miss Alexandra Jentys. Thenceforward the Workers' Committee was the name of the leadership of a local organisation (as far as is known it was in use only in Warsaw and Łódź).

Soon great difficulties, of an ideological and political nature, emerged. Another ideological centre was already in existence. It consisted of the recent Polish emigrés, the members of the Warsaw socialist 'circles' of the late seventies who had escaped arrest and of whom a few, like Waryński, returned to Poland, but of whom most, after spending some time in Austrian and German prisons, settled in Geneva, where they had started to publish first (in 1878) the periodical *Równość*, and after 1881 *Przedświt*. The most important of them were Stanisław Mendelson, Szymon Dikstein, Kazimierz Dłuski and Witold Piekarski. Very soon important divergencies developed between them and the Warsaw leaders of 'Proletariat'. The reasons are not difficult to understand and they were not uniquely Polish. Every political emigration experiences it. In the West it is now fashionable to consider political emigrés as failed politicians, who in time acquire a distorted view of the situation in their native country, which they judge by past knowledge, and whose opinions one should therefore accept with great caution. But history has none of these prejudices about men and their ideas. Political emigrés were sometimes wrong. But often they saw further and more clearly than those who were immersed in their daily work and struggle. And this is true especially when one considers the conditions in which political work has to be carried on in authoritarian countries, where the first element of rational politics, information, is distorted or not available. To take only one or two examples: it cannot be maintained that the Bolshevik leaders who remained in Russia in the summer of 1917 recognised the growing political disintegration of their country better than Lenin, a life-long political emigré, viewing it from his Swiss café, or that the French resistance had a clearer view of Europe than General de Gaulle in London during the War.

In the spring of 1883 Waryński went from Warsaw to Geneva to try to persuade the editors of *Przedświt* to change their line on important matters concerning the policies of 'Proletariat'. In 1883 *Przedświt* was the only Polish socialist paper published in the West, and therefore its editors felt themselves obliged to express all possible opinions and ideas which were circulating among Poles. That meant not only the revolutionary and marxist ideas prevalent in the Russian Kingdom of Poland but also those emerging in Austrian Galicia and German Poznań or Silesia, where the rest of the Poles were living. And although the editors of *Przedświt* came from the Kingdom, they also tried to transplant their socialism into the other parts of partitioned Poland. In doing so they became acquainted with the different political and ideological climates existing in German- and Austrian-ruled countries. Soon, then, marxism in Bismarckian Germany and much more in Franz Joseph's Austro-Hungary was losing its revolutionary virginity and was moving towards evolutionary 'reformist' social democracy. For a time the editors of *Przedświt* still defended the most orthodox marxist interpretation of past history and present events. But perforce, wanting to become the platform of all Polish socialists, in all three parts of partitioned Poland, they had to open their columns to opinions which were not exactly those of the Warsaw 'Proletariat'. In January 1883 the editors announced[21] that they were starting an 'official column' in the paper which would be free from 'editorial censorship', and for which the board 'carried no responsibility'. And they wisely added: 'If we want it [the paper] to do good service [to the cause], then it should not appear to express the views only of *our* group; and above all, if we want not to collide with groups inside the country, a military line is impossible.'

Thus, when for a short time 'Solidarność' was competing with 'Proletariat' for influence among Warsaw socialists, the paper was sympathetically reporting the activities of both organisations even in the same factory. A little later, in October 1883, *Przedświt* (No. 24) called on 'Proletariat' and 'Solidarność' to drop their differences in view of the danger of splitting the young socialist movement, and to unite again to fight 'for one goal'. This was very irritating to the Warsaw leaders of 'Proletariat'. But an even stronger reason for the worsening of relations was the attitude of the majority of the editorial board to the decision of the Wilno conference to recognise the Russian 'Narodnaya Volya' as the leading organisation of all revolutionaries in the Tsarist empire, and to recommend the affiliation to it of 'Proletariat', on a federal basis. At a meeting in May 1883 the editors of *Przedświt* had formally repudiated the idea of the 1881 Letter about the readiness of Polish socialists to form one party with the Russians. They were more sympathetic to the opinion of a Cracow group ('Gmina Krakowska') which in December 1882 had stated that 'our first aim will be the unification with Polish groups from the Russian and Prussian partitions in one Polish socialist party' and that only later should they form federal parties with neighbouring socialists (Russian, Lithuanian, etc.). When the report of the Wilno conference was about to be published in *Przedświt*, the opposition to it among its editors (two against one) was so strong that the part dealing with this question was omitted.[22] Waryński, who had been in Geneva since April trying to win over this important paper to his point of view, failed completely. Disappointed, he went back to Warsaw. However, it looks as though he succeeded in preventing some funds from reaching *Przedświt*, because for a full seven months after his departure the periodical stopped publication.

It was probably under the influence of this political defeat that Waryński decided to sponsor a publication which would be independent of the 'unreliable' comrades writing in the West, and under his personal control, fully express the opinion of 'Proletariat'.

5 TIME OF SUCCESS

ON THE CREST OF THE WAVE

The call of the party to resist the medical inspection of women workers, and the consequent withdrawal of the authorities, had been a great triumph for the young organisation. 'Proletariat', although illegal and poor in personnel and technical means, had at once made itself widely known in society and became popular, especially among workers. It was the only group, with the exception of the Church, which cared for the underprivileged in the industrial towns and settlements, and which had direct contacts with them.

The marxist leaders of 'Proletariat' were unsure about the role the Polish peasantry (the overwhelming majority of the nation) should play in the revolution. At first they considered only the landless peasants, the '*parobki*', the labourers who migrated across the country to find work on the bigger estates, as allies of the industrial working class. But in June 1883 the Central Committee of the party published an appeal ('read it to the illiterate' and 'after reading hand it over to others')[1] under the title: 'Manifesto to those toiling on the land from the Central Committee of the Social Revolutionary Party.' The name 'Proletariat' was omitted. But in small print at the end was added: 'In the printing shop of Proletariat.'

The Manifesto described firstly the desperate economic situation of the peasants after 'the landlords have robbed or cheated you of the land, on which you and your forefathers toiled and made of you their subjects'. But had the Tsar's land reform improved their situation? 'Today only half of you possess anything and only one in five has enough to feed himself.'

The peasants needed land. But neither the Polish landlords nor the Tsar cared for them. As the Manifesto appeared after the coronation, the authors of the appeal described in some detail the great cost of the ceremonies which, they said, had been covered by 'your *grosh* extracted from the land', and by the taxes paid on everything bought in the shops. The Tsar had declared that no more land would be given or sold to peasants. Therefore, said the Manifesto, they must prepare themselves to fight against the Tsar, a struggle which 'may start soon'. Only the socialists would fight for the interest of the peasants and, as 'the city workers will get the *factories*, so will the country revolution give you, peasants, the *land*, and everybody freedom'. The Manifesto ended with the assurance: 'In the moment of the revolution we will be with you; you will recognise us, because only we will tell you: the land ought to belong to those who till it.'

Unlike the Russian Populist socialists, the European marxists had neither then, nor later, worked out a peculiarly socialist answer to the problem of land hunger which afflicted the peasantry in central and eastern Europe. The Polish Manifesto had nothing of a collectivist nature, no appeal to instincts other than those of private ownership and individual possession. It was true to the tradition of all the agrarian reformers in Polish history since the second half of the eighteenth century. And they were certainly not collectivists, or even egalitarians.

The party leadership regarded its appeal to the peasants as being of singular importance. The Manifesto was presented to all town 'circles' as a subject for discussion and clarification. Members were mobilised to distribute the Manifesto in villages and on estates – everywhere where peasants could be approached. Addresses of peasant relatives were collected from workers, and the leaflets were then sent to them by post. A police report[2] mentioned 5,000 leaflets being distributed in such ways, though this is probably an exaggeration. According to the police, the Manifesto was read by peasants in the Warsaw, Piotrków (which included Lódź), Kielce, Siedlce, Kalisz, Lublin and Lomźa *gubernias*. The party published simultaneously a Lithuanian translation of the Manifesto, which was distributed in the Wilno and Suwałki *gubernias*. Any worker or student member of 'Proletariat' who during the summer went on holiday in the country was obliged to take copies of the leaflet with him for distribution. It was the most successful propaganda operation by the young party. Consequently, its mass character could not for long remain undetected by the police. Four members of the party were arrested and the subversive Manifesto was found on them. Much worse was the fact that two members (Innocenty Rutkowski and Władysław Paszkiewicz) betrayed the party and became police agents, informing on the activities and personnel of the illegal organisation. For the first time the police were able to discover who were the people who led the party, and could thus begin to trace its activities.

But for some months to come 'Proletariat' flourished. Its organisational network was growing fast. It had now many branches or contacts outside Warsaw. The most important were in Łódź, Piotrków, Pabianice, Tomaszów Mazowiecki, Zgierz, Żyrardów, Puławy, Białystok, Płock, Kalisz, Częstochowa, Pruszków, Wilno, Grodno, and Pińsk. The party had also student branches in Kiev, Moscow, St Petersburg and Odessa. Abroad its members were active in Geneva, Paris and Leipzig.[3]

It was impossible and dangerous in the conditions of underground work to have a register of names of party members. One can only guess at the number of people who belonged to the party 'circles' and committees, or who took part in its activities in some other way. There were probably between fifteen hundred and two thousand altogether – a very respectable number compared with the number of members in Russian revolutionary organisations, then or even twenty years later.

At the time of publishing the Manifesto to the peasants, the central committee also distributed another short leaflet (dated 15 June 1883),[4] in connection with the coronation on 27 May of 'the blood-soaked executioner, Romanov Alexander the Third'. The leaflet stated that neither the workers nor the peasants, nor even the intelligentsia, although they 'because of their cowardly inclinations do not understand that only the revolution shows the way out from the fatal slavery', had gained anything under Tsardom. Only the gentry and the bourgeoisie saw in the monarchy the defender of their interests. Only 'Proletariat' together 'with the Russian revolutionaries' challenged the system. The struggle should have no nationalist character. 'The time of national separatism has passed, and the idea of freedom must unite all its real friends.' The leaflet ended with a call on everyone to take up 'the historically fixed place' and to fight, and suffer until the day of victory.

All these activities, especially the wide publication and dissemination of the party's points of view, were possible because the organisation had been able to acquire its own printing shop. On the Manifesto, the leaflets, and a little later, on the clandestine periodical which began to appear in the early autumn, an end line always proudly announced: 'In the printing shop of Proletariat.'

It was a very small printing establishment, which was moved around from one place to another, mainly in Warsaw itself, but finally, before it was discovered by the police, to the outskirts so as to escape detection.[5] The people employed in it were devoted party members, but often without even an elementary knowledge of the trade. They worked in constant danger of being caught and severely punished by the police and courts. They were armed with revolvers, knives and knuckledusters to enable them to resist arrest.

The party printing shop was assembled with the help of members of the Russian 'Narodnaya Volya'. The contacts and collaboration of the Polish and Russian revolutionaries was becoming closer than ever before or after. It is a very interesting chapter in the bridge-building consciously undertaken by these two groups who represented the most radical elements among the Russian and Polish peoples.

During his stay in Geneva, one of Waryński's missions was to get in touch with Lev Tikhomirov and Marya Oshanina-Olovienikova, leading members of 'Narodnaya Volya', who were representing the Russian organisation abroad. The Poles were still very eager to push forward their idea of forming one all-Russian revolutionary party, to which 'Proletariat' could affiliate and whose political leadership it would accept. Nothing is known about the course of these Geneva talks. The Russians themselves were then in deep trouble because of the activities of Sergey

Degayev, who played the double role of a revolutionary leader and of a close collaborator with the inspector of the Tsar's political police, Grigory Sudeykin. At this time the whole leadership of 'Narodnaya Volya' was already captured, and none of its lower rank members knew either the source from which the gendarmes got their information or where the next blow would fall.

At this moment in their history the Russian revolutionaries moved a large part of their underground activities to Warsaw, Wilno, Białystok and Grodno. One of the most active of the Narodnovoltsy in Warsaw was the Grodno printer and Pole, Marceli Janczewski. In March 1883 he constructed with the help of Poles three clandestine printing shops, which he transferred to Kharkow, where the secret seat of the leadership of 'Narodnaya Volya' then was. The same Janczewski afterwards proceeded to assemble a printing workshop for the Poles.*

Janczewski organised in Warsaw a strong branch of 'Narodnaya Volya', among whose members were many Polish–Jewish students who simultaneously belonged also to the Polish party 'Proletariat' (e.g. Leon Winawer and Wacław Handelsman). But Polish Roman Catholics also joined the Russian organisation in Warsaw.[6] In April 1883 21-year-old Varvara Shchulepnikova, who officially represented the Russian organisation in its relations with 'Proletariat', settled in Warsaw. At the same time she intensified the activities of her party in the Kingdom. Warsaw became an important place in the Russian organisation. In February the police arrested in Kharkow Vera Figner, the last member of the National Executive living in Russia. Soon afterwards Degayev delivered into the hands of the police the leaders of the central military organisation, Lieutenant-Colonel Mikhail Ashenbrenner and his closest collaborators, two young officers. All active members of 'Narodnaya Volya' and the printing shop were soon seized too. Then there arrived in Warsaw the highly placed revolutionary Galina Tcshernyavskaya on her way to Paris; there she met the Russian Staff-Captain Konstantin Stepurin, whom she persuaded

---

* Janczewski under interrogation first disclosed Waryński's role in 'Proletariat'.

to leave the army and to move to St Petersburg to take over the party leadership and put together its shattered fragments. Her other important mission in Warsaw was to ask 'Proletariat' to delegate some of the Poles' most active members to work in Russia proper. In consequence, two members of the central committee of 'Proletariat', Rechniewski and Dębski, either settled in St Petersburg or frequently visited it. Later, Kunicki joined them in these purely Russian activities.

Not only in Warsaw were there to be found Poles who simultaneously belonged to 'Narodnaya Volya' and to 'Proletariat'. It happened even more frequently in Wilno and Białystok, where many Jewish workers were already active in revolutionary work. When, for example, the St Petersburg printer, Alexander Nikvist, delegated by Degayev, visited Białystok in search of a hiding place, it was Abram Lubnitski, a leader of the local organisations of 'Proletariat' and 'Narodnaya Volya', whose help he received.

In the spring of 1883, as mentioned above, Janczewski, sent by Degayev to Warsaw, assembled there a clandestine printing shop for 'Narodnaya Volya' after the last one had been betrayed to the police by the same Degayev, and soon started producing *Listok Narodnoi Volyi*, the periodical of the party, there.* It was only natural that each of the two revolutionary groups, the Russian and the Polish, would use each other's facilities, and personnel, for their clandestine activities. This was especially true of the conspiratorial addresses used by both organisations in Warsaw, in Białystok and in Wilno. In time, one of the most courageous Russian revolutionaries, the 40-year-old Justice of the Peace Piotr Bardovsky, and Natalia Poll his common-law wife, also a Russian, were to play a most prominent role in the activities of 'Proletariat' and he was to end his life on the gallows, together with three Poles. These were serious times, and these were serious men and women who knew the price they would have to pay for their ideas and their deeds.

* *Listok Narodnoi Volyi* was published from 1881 to 1886. The last issue appeared in November 1886.

THE UNDERGROUND PERIODICAL

By the middle of 1883 the party had two or three small printing shops, which were working in the most primitive technical conditions. Not only was the type-setting done by hands mostly unaccustomed to composing, but so was the printing. The type was either brought in from Russia or smuggled in from Germany and Austria with the help of Social Democrats in those countries. The risks of being detected, and afterwards disappearing into prison or exile, were very considerable. Since the assassination of 1881 the Tsarist gendarmerie had been given wide powers and appropriate means to eradicate any sign of subversion and revolutionary action in the empire. Yet the Poles knew that once they decided to move away from 'propaganda', from pure education, to the 'agitation' stage, the party could no longer base a large part of its activities only on brochures, translated from foreign languages, printed in the West, and smuggled into the Kingdom many months after they had appeared. Political conflict has no patience. Action and reaction must follow each other without a break if results are to be expected. The first successful engagement of the new party in rousing the Warsaw workers against the threat of medical examination by the police of their women comrades was possible because the organisation was able to react to the police announcement at once, only three days after the order appeared in the official gazette. From then on, the short leaflet or manifesto replaced the brochure and booklet.

Ludwik Waryński's unsuccessful journey to Geneva, where he tried, and failed, to make of *Przedświt* the organ of 'Proletariat', strengthened the hands of those of the Warsaw leaders who from the beginning had aimed at launching a periodical which they would control entirely, and which would be written by people on the spot for a local readership. One of the sources of friction between Warsaw and Geneva, the sympathetic reporting in *Przedświt* of the two rival Warsaw organisations, 'Proletariat' and 'Solidarność', disappeared after a few months with the fading away of the latter. But a far more basic problem remained: the question of the attitude of a Polish socialist movement to the national situation. In 1884, when the 'Proletariat' faction at last succeeded in getting a majority in the Geneva group, two members of the editorial board of *Przedświt*, Kazimierz Długski and Witold Piekarski, resigned. The Warsaw delegate, Stanisław Kunicki, reporting the reasons of the split, wrote:[7] 'They do not agree with our relations with the Russians ('Narodnaya Volya'). They want an organisation within ethnographic frontiers.' As the historian, Adam Próchnik, remarks in this connection, it is not clear from the last part of this quotation whether the dissenting members of the board favoured one socialist party embracing all the ethnographically Polish territories irrespective of their existing state borders, or whether they demanded that 'Proletariat' should extend its activities and organisations into the Russian empire as far east as there were larger groups of Poles to be found.[8]

And so it was in Warsaw between September 1883 and May 1884 that the most important publication representing the evolving views of the new party appeared. It described itself as the 'organ of the International, Social Revolutionary Party'. And the periodical called itself, as did the party, *Proletariat*. Above the main title it had on the left-hand side the words: 'Freedom, Factories, Land!' And on the right: 'Workers of all countries unite!' Under the main heading it called on its readers: 'Defenders of the Workers' Cause, distribute this paper!'

No price was given, for the paper was not sold to its readers, but it was expected that its recipients would donate something to party funds.

Before the Second World War there existed, as far as is known, three complete collections of this paper. Two of them were destroyed during the War and only one survived, which now belongs to the Marx–Engels–Lenin Institute in Moscow. In 1957 a reprint of the paper was published in Warsaw, based on photostats of the Moscow copy.

All in all, five issues of *Proletariat* appeared in the course of eight months. The sixth issue was prepared for publication, but it never appeared in print because the police discovered and seized the party's secret printing shop in Warsaw, and a little later

arrested in Łódź the Central Committee's agent, Hilary Gostkiewicz, who had been sent there with all the manuscripts for
this issue, to find a shop that would print it.[9]

The five issues which were printed and which were widely
distributed not only in the Kingdom, but also in those parts
of Poland given to Austria and Germany under the partition,
appeared on the following dates: No. 1 on 15 September 1883,
No. 2 on 1 October 1883, No. 3 on 20 October 1883, No. 4 on
20 November 1883, and then, after an interval of five months, the
last issue, No. 5, appeared on 1 May 1884.[10]

The first three issues of *Proletariat* looked like any normal
daily newspaper, each page being divided into three columns.
Each issue consisted of four pages. The proof-reading was ex-
cellent, a great achievement considering that it was set secretly by
non-printers whose state of mind can be imagined when one
remembers that they were all armed, ready at any moment to
fight to the death in case of a police raid. The paper was good;
only the printing ink used in the first three issues was very
inferior. After three issues the size of the paper was reduced, to
make it easier to read inconspicuously. The layout of the fifth
and last issue of *Proletariat* was radically changed, being printed
on much thinner paper and with a much narrower format than
before. But instead of the four pages it had eighteen. It was much
better suited for keeping even in a small pocket or inside a
seemingly innocuous book. On the last page the last line, as in
every issue, was: 'In the party's printing shop.'

The editorial material of all five issues can be divided into
three main groups. One part was devoted to a leading article on a
political subject on which the party wanted to express its opinion
or make people take action. In the same section were articles
which developed the party's attitude to other classes in Polish
society, to the Russian revolutionaries of 'Narodnaya Volya', to
the government, to strikes, to war and peace, to anti-semitism
and to the international labour movement. Developments in
Russia were also given a prominent place in the paper. Another
group of articles described conditions in particular factories,
in Warsaw and the provinces, in villages and abroad. These

included reports on Polish life under the Habsburgs and Hohenzollerns, and in Western countries with strong socialist and trade union movements. But the largest part of the periodical was devoted to organisational matters. In each issue the Central Committee of the party published its appeals and instructions. A most important part of these columns were warnings about police spies and the exposure of agents-provocateurs whose names and private addresses were given and also the places where they pursued their pernicious activities. Arrests of persons accused by the police of socialist connections were also published in this section of the paper. Sometimes the names of factory-owners and managers, whose behaviour towards their workers was considered exceptionally obnoxious, were given, together with warnings about the consequences of their behaviour. For example, in the third issue of *Proletariat* we find a communiqué 'from the Central Committee' announcing the 'carrying out of the death sentence* on Szremski', a textile worker in Zgierz, who allegedly denounced members of the party to the police. The communiqué closed with the sentence: 'The same punishment will befall every traitor-spy and informer'. In nearly every issue of the paper were reports of donations to the funds of the party (only the initials or nicknames of the donors were given). The party's Red Cross reported not only contributions but also expenses, especially the amount of money paid out to the families of arrested comrades. Then came small advertisements about party booklets as well as publications of 'Narodnaya Volya'. Announcements about the death of comrades, whose names were printed between black lines, appeared regularly.

Another column in the paper consisted of revolutionary or satirical poems (the text of the famous 'Warszawianka' was published in the first issue of the periodical), and twice there appeared short stories which painted the miserable life of workers, and the revolutionary response of the best of them.

Ludwik Waryński, who put all his energy and enthusiasm into building up the underground printing shop which enabled the young party to publish its own regular periodical in Warsaw, was

* In reality he was only slightly wounded.

one of the very few leaders of 'Proletariat' who could write articles and edit the work of others so as to make it readable. As Adam Próchnik, a historian of the Polish socialist movement, writes:[11] 'In the beginning the only intellectuals in Warsaw... were Waryński and Puchewicz. Soon the latter left to form a new party ['Solidarność'] and attracted to himself a group of young people.' The 'legal' marxists like Krusiński did not contribute to the illegal *Proletariat*. Waryński found only one other person, Edmund Płoski, to help him in editing the periodical. But that arrangement lasted only a few weeks, because after preparing and printing the second issue of *Proletariat* both of them were arrested by the police.

Fortunately there arrived at the same time in Warsaw a group of students and graduates (Tadeusz Rechniewski, Alexander Dębski, Stanisław Kunicki) from universities in Russia who filled the empty places as editors and article writers in the periodical. But as Kunicki made clear in a letter which he wrote in the summer of 1884 to Waryński, then in a cell of the Tenth Pavilion of the Warsaw Citadel (the letter never reached him),[12] 'Everything is all right but for the horrible lack of literary ability – we hope that this will emerge from among the youth here, but this needs time; and now we are able only with great difficulty to publish an issue once a month. We want to bring somebody from abroad.' Indeed, the best writers the Polish socialists then had were concentrated round *Przedświt* in Geneva, to which in 1884 was added *Walka Klas*, which was addressed to less sophisticated readers. This fact in no way diminishes the role which the Warsaw periodical played, not only in the Kingdom of Poland, where it was distributed and widely read while the ink on it was still fresh, but also among the emigrés. It may have been less brilliantly written, but it had authenticity and directness of language, especially in its reports from factories and workers' suburbs, owing to the editors' personal contacts and experience. The five published issues of *Proletariat*, and the sixth which survived in manuscript form in the archives of the Tsarist political police, are therefore more than a paper: they are also an important political and sociological document.

The editors of the periodical were full of contempt for all
those in their society who did not share their political and social
ideas. 'We care little how the general public will receive us',
they wrote in the opening article of the first issue. They saw the
Polish nation as consisting of only one progressive class – the
workers. All others were condemned by history, and the revolutionaries, and were soon to perish as a part of the international
class of exploiters. The reactionary classes consisted, as the editors
saw them, not only of the land-owning gentry and the bourgeoisie,
but also of the 'bourgeois-gentry intelligentsia', of whom only a
tiny group became the allies of the proletariat. In the villages,
where the overwhelming majority of Poles lived in the early
eighties, the socialists looked forward to winning over 'the
peasant proletariat', admitting that 'until lately – we must confess
[the movement] has made very little progress'. In an article 'Our
slogan', printed in the second issue of *Proletariat*, the author was
ready to admit that the lower classes of the nation were patriotic,
but because of that they were always cheated by the ruling
groups who raised the insurgents' banner for the sake of 'the
prolongation of privileges handed down by history'. Thus, said
the article, in reality 'our society was therefore not revolutionary'.
But anyway the former 'knights of the sword have changed into
the knights of...capital'. The worker had 'turned away with
disgust from this "historical treasury" [of patriotism]' and now
gathered 'round the banner: "Down with the Poland of the
gentry and bourgeoisie! Long live the international social,
working class republic!"'

This was language never before used by Poles against their
own patriots. It was crude in its generalisations. Not all former
insurgents had become dull and self-satisfied 'knights of capital'.
The socialist paper was read by the more intelligent workers
and younger members of the intelligentsia. One of the leading
members of 'Proletariat', writing about this period forty years
later, made the revealing comment that although there was no
organised movement of patriotic socialists, this was only because
'nobody bothered' to organise those workers who 'were patriots'.[13]
Underground movements give great power to those who happen

to occupy their commanding heights. If 'Proletariat' had not been destined to be crushed in such a relatively short time, there can be no doubt that this extreme rejection of history, sentiments and political reality would have brought about a reaction which would have resulted in a radical revision of its ideology or in a deep split, as in fact happened in a later phase of the Polish labour movement. The interpretation of recent Polish history strictly according to the class content of society must, when it was first made by the early Polish marxists, have been attractive to all those who saw romantic patriotism shattered by its repeated defeats. Its social analysis may now seem to us to have been based on too little understanding of the spiritual forces which determined the stand taken by different groups of Polish society on the national question. The political deductions which the first Polish marxists, and their ideological heirs in the Social Democratic Party of the Kingdom of Poland and Lithuania (SDKPiL) or the Communist Party of Poland, made from their rigid theories condemned them to half a century of political isolation and impotence. But at the same time it give them a distinctive position, which in the eyes of Stalin and other Russian leaders made them at the end of the Second World War sufficiently trustworthy to be appointed the rulers of a pro-Soviet Poland.*

The rejection of Polish patriotism and the opposition, often taking extreme forms, to any resurrection of an independent state went hand in hand with open admiration for the Russian revolutionary movement. In every issue of *Proletariat* there were articles and notices devoted to the 'heroic deeds' of the Russian comrades. The praise was unconditional. Their activities were

---

* In my next instalment of the history of Polish marxism I hope to describe the complicated relations which existed before the First World War between the Luxemburg leadership of the Polish Social Democratic Party (SDKPiL) and Lenin's Bolsheviks, and the tensions between the inter-war Polish Communist Party (KPP) and Stalin, which ended in the massacre of the Polish leadership during the purges in the late thirties and the formal liquidation of the KPP in 1938 by an ukase of the Comintern. At the end of the Second World War the remnants of the party were utterly dependent on the Soviet army and the N.K.V.D., and thus from Stalin's point of view the right instrument to implement his political plans in Poland.

presented to the Poles as a shining example of how revolutionaries should behave. The illegal publications of Narondovoltsy were recommended to the Poles in the same way as the booklets and leaflets of 'Proletariat'. And although by the time 'Proletariat' appeared the Russian revolutionary movement was already sinking into the morass of internal demoralisation and police provocation, the enthusiasm of the leaders of the Polish socialists for their eastern comrades persisted with the intensity of a first love affair.

Proletariat had, of course, no time for the Tsarist government, which it characterised as 'the most despotic of all the European governments' (in No. 5, 'We and the government'). Its declared aim was to 'break up the administrative organisation, thus demolishing the organised obstacle which stands on the road to our goals'. It considered that victory would be attained only by 'handing over to the leadership of one central organisation the political struggle' against the Tsar's ministers. The Polish socialists thus declared themselves ready to fulfil their revolutionary task as part of the general movement in Russia, led by a 'centralised organisation', which would naturally consist mostly, if not exclusively, of Russians.

Yet, when it came to a serious social and political analysis of what the Tsarist government represented, the leaders of 'Proletariat' were much less inclined to think only in the black or white terms they usually resorted to when they dealt with their own society. They wrote in the article already quoted above that the Russian 'government is the defender of the possessing classes and hence we must fight them!' But they knew too much about the personnel and policies of the administration to put on it a simple class label. They knew that no one class of Russian society was in complete agreement with the government. As they said 'the government's despotism is felt by *all*** social classes'. They went even further. 'The Russian government is not, to be exact, representative of any class. Based chiefly on the bureaucracy and the army, it adopts varying attitudes in differing circumstances, having in mind only its own interest.'

* My italics – L.B.

This was a more serious attempt to understand Russian political reality than the early Polish marxists ever made in relation to their own nation. What they said about the autonomous role of the Tsarist régime *vis-à-vis* other classes and groups was utterly different from the dogmatic marxist view that every government was nothing more than the 'executive committee' of the social class which at that moment of history controlled the economic fabric, and means of production, of its nation or state. But it made sense, and was in harmony with the opinions of most Russians who thought and wrote about it.* There were two possible explanations. One was that the Polish marxists were much more emotionally involved in the ideological battle which they conducted with their own compatriots, who were very often their fathers, brothers and closest personal friends, than when they sat down to describe the Tsarist régime, which must have appeared to them both soulless and utterly impersonal. One has also the strong impression that these young men, who were either still studying in St Petersburg and Moscow, or had just left the centres of Russian political and intellectual life, often knew more about the Russians than about the social life of their own compatriots. The author of the articles quoted above which appeared in two issues of *Proletariat* (No. 4, dated 20 November 1883, and No. 5 of 1 May 1884) was Tadeusz Rechniewski, whose father, a lawyer, practised in St Petersburg. There the young Tadeusz grew up, and in St Petersburg's University he began to study law and to mix with Polish and Russian socialists. Even when writing the most important articles for *Proletariat*, and after becoming its editor on Waryński's arrest in September 1883, he still lived in the Russian capital, from which he often travelled to Warsaw. Rechniewski's background was typical of that of most leaders of 'Proletariat'. It certainly helped them to see the 'Polish problem' in a wider setting. But it also made them less sensitive to the processes of thought and sentiments of their compatriots, whose backgrounds were not the smoke-filled rooms

* The Poles in this case accepted the generally held view of most Russian Populists and especially of P. N. Tkachev, who had very good and close relations with many Polish revolutionaries.

of Russian students but the still not forgotten horrors of a lost national battle.

But whatever the intellectual reaction of the early Polish marxists to the patriotic tradition of the nation, and indeed of their own class (they were nearly all the sons of gentry), they were far from being 'desiccated machines', who coldly rationalised every human or social phenomenon. Every issue of *Proletariat* bore witness to their humanity. They felt for all those who were caught in the machine of the early, mostly primitive and brutal, processes of the industrial revolution in Poland; who led the miserable life of helpless and illiterate peasants, suddenly uprooted from their natural small communities and transferred to town slums. The leaders of 'Proletariat' knew about the early successes which trade unionism had brought to the workers in Britain, in Belgium and Germany, and wrote about it in their periodical. But the stupidity of the government and the blindness of the new rich made it impossible to follow the Western way of improving the living conditions of the new Polish working class. Severe penalties awaited those who tried to organise workers in defence of even their most elementary rights. Trade unionism in the Russia of the nineteenth century was still a criminal conspiracy, to be eradicated by all means at the disposal of the police and the courts. As we said earlier, Waryński at first tried to organise 'Resistance Funds' to support workers who struck or who were sacked because of their industrial militancy. But soon he and his friends in the leadership of 'Proletariat' either lost patience with a slow, uphill movement, or became disillusioned with the pitiable results of quasi-trade union action. In their periodical they soon began to propagate what they called 'economic terror'. As mentioned before, they published names of factory owners and foremen who behaved in a more than usually offensive manner toward their workers, and warned them of the personal consequences of their conduct. The fourth issue of *Proletariat* contained a characteristic short story under the title 'Strike' (its author was the 17-year-old schoolboy Feliks Kon). It told of a strike which was nearing collapse because the workers could no longer bear to see their children suffering hunger and their wives and sisters being assaulted by the soldiery who arrived to defend the greedy factory owner. But just then, like a *deus ex machina*, an unknown man appeared among the workers and in a passionate speech called on them to give up the ineffectual strike weapon and leave it to him, the representative of 'the organisation', to take vengeance on the capitalist and the military. A moment later the whole factory, with the soldiers who garrisoned it against the strikers, turned into fire and ashes, destroyed by a mighty bomb planted by the unknown revolutionary. Some weeks later, we are told in the story, the owner, still shaken by this experience, humbly invited the workers to return to the rebuilt factory, increasing their wages and promising them legal immunity from the consequences of having taken part in a conspiracy and riot.

The moral of the story was clear: in the present conditions only violence on the part of individual revolutionaries would improve the lot of the workers. It should be added that the romantic dream of 'the organisation', the party, frightening the capitalists and the government to make them yield to workers' demands or to force them with the help of individual terrorism, never really materialised in the lifetime of 'Proletariat'. It only provided one more spur to the political administration who when this article was published had already made its plans to liquidate 'Proletariat', its leaders and its active rank and file.

'Proletariat' accepted in theory the principle that terrorism was a legitimate weapon against a tyrannical government. But it was chary of following all the way the theory and practice of 'Narodnaya Volya', which considered that every civil servant, every policeman and army officer individually shared the moral and political responsibility of the system they served, or which employed them, and therefore became a legitimate target for revolutionary vengeance. One or two of the leaders of 'Proletariat' (Kunicki was certainly one of them) probably shared these views. But the majority of the early Polish socialists refused to fight on such a wide front, afraid of the human suffering to which such a generalisation must lead. It was only when the single-minded Józef Piłsudski became the leader of the 'fighting squads' of the Polish Socialist Party in 1904–6 that one faction of the Polish labour movement started practising mass terrorism against each and every individual who was even in the smallest degree connected with the Moscow administration.

The editors of *Proletariat* were very sensitive to the accusations made against the Polish socialists by some of their opponents that there were anti-semitic skeletons in their revolutionary cupboard. After the assassination of Alexander II in March 1881 a wave of anti-Jewish pogroms hit the western territories of the empire, the pale, where the Jewish population was concentrated. The assaults were inspired and in some places directly organised by members of the administration. But 'Narodnaya Volya', already in decline, decided to use the anti-semitic sentiments of the most illiterate part of the population for revolutionary purposes, and published one or two pamphlets in this spirit. In 1883, when the economic crisis spreading over the whole of Europe reached the Kingdom of Poland, bringing with it unemployment for many, and lower wages for the rest, shops and workshops belonging to Jews were attacked and looted. The most violent assaults on Jews occurred in the fast-growing textile centres, in Łódź and Białystok, and even cost lives.

In three of the five issues of *Proletariat* there were articles in which the use of anti-semitism as a weapon in political struggle was unconditionally condemned.

In the first issue, dated 15 September 1883, the anonymous author of an article about Austria described how the 'Hungarian bourgeoisie and gentry in order to hide their own iniquities had now raised the banner of anti-semitism'. These people accused the Jews of being the exploiters of the people while in reality, said the author, 'like every other nationality [the Jews] have been divided into different classes where beside the rich was the wretched proletariat, beside the exploiters – the exploited'. And yet they were made 'the sacrificial goat of the gentry's intrigue and the people's vengeance because they were Jews'. The article protested against 'the tradition [which] until now has maintained the contempt for the Jewish tribe, his depravation of human dignity'. After describing in detail the 'anti-Jewish intrigue' the article stated that, while sympathising with any movement against economic exploitation and political sub-jugation, 'we are filled with disgust when the impulse for that [protest] is tribal hatred and deeply rooted religious prejudices, which were always inimical to the interests of the working class'.

A month later, in the third issue of *Proletariat* dated 20 October 1883, reporting on the struggle of the Irish people against the government in London, and the danger that it might lose its proper aims, the author wrote: 'The assaults on Jews which are now multiplying in Europe are also a movement – but a per-verse movement – much more useful to the enemies of the people than to the people themselves.'

The leaders of the party knew from their close contacts with the workers how real was the danger of anti-semitic outbreaks in Poland. The next issue of their periodical (No. 4 dated 20 November 1883) opened with a leading article which was entirely devoted to anti-semitism. It accused the 'police gazettes' of spreading lies about recently arrested socialists, as being 'anti-semitic agitators'. Nothing of this kind was true, said *Proletariat*. It was the gendarmerie, the police and their 'journalistic lackeys' who were frightened by the thought that 'now the workers are acting against us, against the government, against the factory owners and landlords. Let's turn them against the Jews, and thus maybe escape the tempest.' 'But', continued the article, 'they are mistaken. The socialists have to move on difficult, dim roads – but they aim for light. They want real light for all toilers, without exception, they want all that which knowledge, which experience, which struggles lasting thousands of years have achieved and which only a handful now enjoys.' The socialists would welcome, 'as brothers' every worker, to whatever nation or creed he might belong, in the struggle 'against all exploiters'. They assumed that 'also the Polish workers will not act differently, cannot act differently' because 'they understand...that among the Jewish masses too there are not a few exploited workers, poor as they themselves are, unhappy as they'. The article ended with the words: 'And when the bourgeois [and] police newspapers, when the voices of the patrons of the working class whisper in their ears: "Down with the Jews" – they will always be able to answer: "Down with the capitalists, down with the present capitalist system!"'

'Proletariat' called itself the 'International Social Revolutionary Party', and by words and deeds testified its loyalty to the first adjective in its title. It abhorred any chauvinism, any hatred of people because they belonged to a different nation or adhered to another religious creed (it is of interest to note that, conscious of the deep devotion of the Polish workers to the Christian religion and the Roman Catholic Church, the marxist leaders of the party kept their atheist convictions to themselves, never publicly criticised religion or attacked its representatives). They collaborated openly with Russians and recommended their literature, in the Russian language, to the Polish workers. Because in Łódź and its environs there were many German workers, *Proletariat* translated some of its publications into that language. German-speaking workers joined 'Proletariat', as did Russians living in the Kingdom, and Jewish workers in Białystok and Wilno, whose language was Yiddish.

Yet, like so many socialists then (but not Marx) they felt lost, and frightened, when the situation demanded that they should declare themselves on matters concerning the relations between states. Foreign policy looked to them like a quagmire which could easily drown their socialist purity. Writing about the danger of a war between Russia and Austro-Hungary because of the latter's economic infiltration of the Balkans, which the Tsar's government considered a Russian domain, Waryński declared (in the second issue of *Proletariat*, dated 1 October 1883) the socialists' utter neutrality in any conflict between states and governments. He saw no basic difference in the peoples' living conditions in either of these states. In a way his attitude was the same as that which Lenin adopted forty years later.

In general we ought to avoid foreign policy like a swamp, because in it more than one cause has got stuck ... when the call to war will be sounded among us ... and when they [the masses] will start moving, then we will join them not to allow the political imposters to use this force for their villainous aims ... Let them [the masses] march, but under our banners!!!

When these words reached the readers of the periodical, Waryński was already a prisoner, never again to breathe the air of freedom. More than any other of his contemporaries among Polish socialists he had the ability to look ahead, and the talent to present a complicated intellectual argument in the simple language of a working-class propagandist.

The fifth number of *Proletariat*, dated 1 May 1884, was the final issue of the underground periodical of the party.[13] The conspirators who organised the secret printing shop were young and had little practical training for this kind of work. The working conditions were, understandably, the worst possible. The food consisted often of bread and tea for days. Yet the illegal printing shop of the party produced not only some 15,000 copies of *Proletariat*, but also many leaflets and two pamphlets (one of which was a translation into Polish of Piotr Kropotkin's *To the Young*)[14] in many thousands of copies. The police did for some time have informers among the lower ranks of the party, and were in possession of copies of the 'subversive' publications. On 28 September 1883 Ludwik Waryński was caught by the police. In the next few days the police searched many houses looking for the printing shop. Yet it survived for a full eighteen months; it was moved from one place to another.

It was only on 25 October 1884 that the gendarmes succeeded in discovering it. A group of young party members tried afterwards to assemble another printing shop where the sixth issue of *Proletariat* was to be printed. But before this could happen the new printing shop was also seized by the police (September 1885). The party agent Gostkiewicz was then sent to Łódź to try to print there, but he was arrested, and the manuscript confiscated.[15] Thus the fifth issue ended the history of the periodical.

The five issues of *Proletariat* gave the most reliable, and fullest, account of the way the leaders of the party thought on matters which were of great concern to them. We say 'leaders' because, judging the internal life of 'Proletariat' on the basis of the memories of its members and the documents and acts drawn up by the police and investigating judges, one is left with the definite impression that the intellectual gap existing then between

H

the intelligentsia and the working-class members of the party precluded a high degree of ideological collaboration. We must not forget either that the party was illegal, that its peak period was in the time of the repression after Alexander's assassination, which was certainly not conducive to any leisurely intellectual exercises between active revolutionaries and their rank and file followers, who were quite unprepared for theoretical discussions. But this does not mean that the ideas of Waryński, Rechniewski, Puchewicz, Dębski and Kunicki were the esoteric creation of a few, and had no influence on the many. They established the marxist tradition in the Polish labour movement* which survived even the Stalinist period in spite of the blunders and stupidities of so many of its representatives. Their rejection of chauvinism and nationalism made them blind to the natural aspirations of a people with a long state history and of a burning love for their country. But it was a necessary correction to the egocentrism which made some Poles put their nationalism above the higher laws of humanity. Their analysis of the motives which made so many of their compatriots, earlier and later, sacrifice their lives for the idea of an independent Poland was in most cases sub-jectively very unjust. Yet the fact remains that most of them were either unwilling to let new classes move up to lead the nation or lacked the vision and determination needed to build a bridge between the class to which they belonged and the vast majority of the nation. The rationalism of the early (and later) Polish marxists was extreme and exaggerated. But it was a healthy reaction against the superficial romanticism so widely prevalent and which brought so many bitter defeats to the Poles in the nineteenth century. Nevertheless, it would be unfair to blame only the opponents of marxism in Polish society for surrendering to dreams in politics, and not to notice the naivety of the men of 'Proletariat' who uncritically admired a mythological Revolution and saw in the International (dead and already buried because of the feud between the anarchists and marxists) the divine in-

---

* The curious fact is that in no issue of the periodical is Marx's name ever mentioned. Waryński and his colleagues probably never forgave him for the support he gave to the movements for the resurrection of a Polish state.

strument for the progress and renovation of the human race. Their mistakes had all to do with the untried future, while most of their opponents were still bound to the receding past. In their active compassion for those millions of their compatriots who were suffering the indignities of traditional poverty in the villages and the misery of a young, greedy new industrial society, they had no peers, apart from a few sensitive writers and some members of the lower clergy. While the marxist-revolutionary ideas of the first Polish socialist party became the inheritance of only a minority of the later labour movement, the spirit of indignation against social injustice which they expressed with so much passion became the legacy of the whole of the Left in Polish society.

6 TIME OF TERROR

For a full twelve months, between September 1882 and September 1883, the party, although illegal, was able to recruit many members in factories and universities without much interference by the authorities. As we have seen, its propaganda efforts were considerable: it published the programme Manifesto, as well as leaflets and pamphlets, and in September 1883 it successfully started the printing and distribution of the periodical *Proletariat*, ambitiously intended to appear as a fortnightly. The mass action in February of that year to defend the women workers against the humiliating personal health checks ordered by the police, was the first political confrontation which the Tsarist authorities had had to deal with in the Kingdom of Poland since the suppression of the insurrection of 1863-4. The fact that the government had to withdraw the order under the pressure of an outraged public opinion, which in this case supported the revolutionaries, must have seriously disturbed the secret police department which was responsible for keeping order among the Polish subjects of the Tsar. Preventive action had to be taken.

The records of the proceedings of the trial of twenty-nine leaders of the party, which took place in December 1885 in Warsaw, show that the police had begun to prepare their case against the revolutionary Polish organisation as early as February 1883.[1] Even if the leaders and rank and file of 'Proletariat' had been more experienced in evading police spies, even if they had shown less bravado and more prudence, the result would still have been the same. Their forces were so much weaker than those of the mighty Russian state. Most of their members were first generation urban workers untrained in the art of conspiracy. The leaders were young enthusiasts, who saw martyrdom as an unavoidable stage in the pioneering period of revolutionary socialism. They were also too trusting.

The first blow fell rather by accident. On 28 September 1883, preoccupied with the preparations for printing the second issue of the party periodical, Ludwik Waryński went to the centre of Warsaw (now Dzierżyński Square) where he was to meet a delegate of the executive committee of 'Narodnaya Volya', Varvara Shchulepnikova, who had just arrived from Russia. On the way he stopped for a moment in a shop in the same building to buy some stamps. After leaving the shop and posting his letter he suddenly remembered that he had left behind a parcel consisting of prints of the song 'Warszawianka', which appeared in the first issue of *Proletariat*. It was too late. In the meantime the shopkeeper had opened the parcel and sent a friend to inform the police about the unexpected discovery. Waryński, who was personally unknown to the shopkeeper, instead of leaving the compromising package to its fate and quickly changing the place of the rendezvous, returned to the shop to retrieve it, and went with it into the coffee house where Shchulepnikova was already waiting for him. A moment later a police officer, accompanied by a civilian, burst in and tried to arrest Waryński, who resisted, but was nevertheless seized. This gave the Russian revolutionary time to escape, and warn the leaders of the party of the arrest of Waryński. Although Waryński was then using false papers (as an Austrian subject with the name of Karol Postol, a lithographic worker)[2] he was identified the same evening. The police had already employed professional informers among the Warsaw workers, some of whom had penetrated the party organisation, and there were also those who, when arrested while distributing revolutionary leaflets, easily broke under investigation and gave away everything they knew. Most of these knew Waryński, who had never spared himself.

Although the alarm had been given, the police were able in the next few days to arrest two leading members of 'Proletariat': Edmund Płoski, a member of its Central Committee, and a teacher in the Russian Institute for Nobly Born Ladies in Warsaw, Alexandra Jentys, who was a close personal friend of

Waryński (after his trial he asked the prison authorities for permission to marry her, but was refused). Alexandra Jentys's flat in the Institute was the secret party office. But fortunately she was able to keep the police investigators in ignorance of her real name for three days, during which a woman friend of hers, a member of 'Proletariat', went to her room and removed the most incriminating documents and the correspondence between the Central Committee and its 'agents' in other towns and cities, and also with the student groups in Russia proper. From 2 October 1883 until July 1884 the headquarters of 'Proletariat' was set up in the flat of the Russian judge, Piotr Bardovsky. He, and his common-law wife, Natalia Poll, both sympathisers with 'Narodnaya Volya', played a very important role by helping to keep the Polish underground organisation intact in spite of the growing wave of police persecution.[3]

After the arrests in September and early October only three members of the party's Central Committee were left free: Stanisław Kunicki, Tadeusz Rechniewski and Henryk Dulęba, the only working-class member of the leadership (although also of gentle origin). During the next ten months, until the police discovered their identity and arrested them, they directed the activities of the party. The most prominent among them was the twenty-two-year-old Stanisław Kunicki.

His background, character, and temperament played a decisive role in the next and almost the final chapter in the history of 'Proletariat' as a mass party of socialist intelligentsia and workers. It is therefore of interest briefly to recount his biography.[4] He was born in 1861 in Tiflis. His father, a Pole, was then serving in the Russian garrison as a doctor, holding the rank of Colonel. His mother was a Georgian. He was brought up in Russia and spoke Polish badly.[5] In 1881 he joined 'Narodnaya Volya' while studying in St Petersburg. There he also joined the Polish group of socialist students. Waryński persuaded him to join 'Proletariat' in 1883. His contemporary, Feliks Kon, who knew him well, said that Kunicki joined the revolutionary movement because he was attracted 'more to the form than the essence, to the external rather than the internal: to the secrecy, conspiracy, with the accessories of a plot'.[6] Kon continued: 'For the sake of an external effect Kunicki was ready to sacrifice much.'[7] 'A typical Narodnovolets' who did not know Polish social conditions too well.[8] But what he lacked in knowledge, prudence and experience Kunicki made up in great personal courage. He was a bad judge of men;* but he also made people follow him wherever he wished.

In October 1883, in the days and weeks after the arrest of Waryński and his closest collaborators, Kunicki, who was known to the police because of his Russian activities, had to go into hiding in St Petersburg. For a short while Rechniewski and Dulęba led the party.

The Warsaw arrests were a great blow to the party. Others soon followed in the provinces. They came first in Łódź, where 'Proletariat' had a lively organisation consisting only of factory workers. One of them betrayed the organisation to the police and arrests followed.[9] But of much greater consequence for the future fate of 'Proletariat' was the treachery of the textile worker Józef Śremski, a member of the party organisation in Zgierz. In September 1883 he denounced three of his comrades as active revolutionaries. For the first time since its existence the Central Committee in Warsaw took the decision to 'eliminate' a police spy. The sentence was confirmed by the local members. On 14 October a party member, Jozef Szmaus, attacked Śremski in the street with a knife. Śremski, slightly wounded, was able to pursue his assailant who was caught red-handed by passers-by.[10] From then on the government was able to hand over arrested members of the party to the tender mercies of the Military Tribunals, accusing them not just of subversive propaganda, but also of criminal acts. The punishment in such case was death on the gallows for those directly involved and slow death in the harshest conditions (in Schlisselburg fortress or in the Siberian mines) for those who took an indirect part in promoting terrorist acts.

The arrests of Waryński, Płoski, Alexandra Jentys, and other

---

* He appointed as an 'agent first class' in the party Stanisław Pacanowski, who thus was in possession of all its secrets. But as soon as Pacanowski was arrested he confessed fully to the police, revealing every detail of its activities.

leading members of the party, the growing penetration by police spies of the local organisations, the lack of any experience in answering questions by interrogators, gave the prosecutor's office in Warsaw enough essential information to plan a major assault on the underground mass organisations, the so-called 'Workers' Circles', which were active in many of the larger Warsaw factories. On the night of 31 October the gendarmerie and police, supplied with a list of forty names of workers suspected of belonging to 'Proletariat's' Circles, were arrested in their homes, which were thoroughly searched. Platoons of Cossacks under the command of the gendarmerie encircled workers' districts and searched every passer-by for illegal publications. At least twenty-one of the most active members of the party, many of them the leaders of the Workers' Circles, were arrested.[11] Those who escaped were too frightened to proceed with their revolutionary activities. With the exception of two or three all the Circles immediately disintegrated. For two or three years the party was still able to count on much sympathy among the workers, but its mass organisation was smashed by the autumn of 1883.

By this time the Central Committee instead of the original seven consisted only of two members: Henryk Dulęba and Alexander Dębski, who was urgently summoned from St Petersburg, being at this time a fervent admirer of the terrorist 'Narodnaya Volya'. It was he who wrote the party leaflet which appeared, dated 9 November 1883 and was signed: 'Warsaw Workers' Committee'.[12] It was printed on the underground presses of *Proletariat* which the gendarmerie, in spite of intensive search, had still been unable to locate. The leaflet ascribed the police raids on workers' quarters and the arrests of 'hundreds of innocent people' to revenge by the 'Polish... factory owners and the Russian government thugs' for the successful launching of the party's periodical which 'has to lead us towards the international social revolution'. Yet, said the authors, 'we will not be intimidated, our energy will not weaken for a moment'. They called on the workers to redouble their struggle. They ended the leaflet with these words: 'Our answer to arrests, searches, will be to double our energy and caution – for traitors and oppressors we will prepare the dagger.'

In this last sentence the new leadership of 'Proletariat' made clear the changed attitude of the party to individual terrorism. In its former pronouncements on this subject violence was to be used only against police spies and traitors. This time the target was widened to include all 'oppressors', a loose definition for marxist revolutionaries. It was soon interpreted as a call and a pledge to attack physically on the widest possible front all enemies of the party and of the workers: the police, government officials combating revolutionary movements, factory owners and managers. It was worse than folly, considering the physical weakness of the party, its lack of means to implement its threats and the reluctance of the public to shelter the perpetrators.* Yet the fact that only a week or so after the mass arrests a printed leaflet issued by 'Proletariat' appeared, and was widely circulated, undoubtedly made a great impression on many. The mysterious leadership of the party seemed not only to be able to survive in spite of all actions taken by the police, but as the leaflet showed, were in spite of the losses full of defiance and confidence. This feeling was only strengthened when on 20 October the third issue of the periodical appeared, to be followed exactly a month later, on 20 November, by the fourth issue of *Proletariat*. The prison cells for those accused of subversive political activities in the dreaded Tenth Pavilion of the Warsaw Citadel were filling up with the leaders and rank-and-file members of 'Proletariat'. Some of them were starting to break down under the strain of intense investigations. But outside, among sympathisers and even opponents, the belief was strong that the revolutionary socialists had a powerful secret organisation, which was led by highly intelligent and extremely able men who would always easily outwit the 'stupid' gendarmes who did not even understand the language of the native population.

But in reality the situation of the party was most precarious. The primitive underground presses had to be moved to yet

---

* In nearly every case of terrorist attacks, the police were able to arrest the guilty only because civilian passers-by helped them in the chase.

another place because it was nearly certain that agents provocateurs had discovered their address. The installation of the party secretariat and archives in the flat of the Russian judge, Piotr Bardovsky, and his wife, Natalia Poll, in the very centre of official Warsaw, was probably the most impressive and dearly-bought manifestation of the solidarity of Russian and Polish revolutionaries who, in spite of the bitter history of their nations, established a completely new tradition on the extreme left of both societies, which no-one who was not poisoned by the fumes of chauvinism would not welcome.

Bardovsky, according to contemporary accounts,[13] was highly respected as a member of the judiciary by all who came in contact with him. During his trial with other members of 'Proletariat' in December 1885 a witness for the prosecution, Agaton Zagórski, who before his arrest and confessions was practically a member of the party's Central Committee, stated that from the late autumn of 1883 Bardovsky's flat had been the central point of the Polish leadership's activities. There the Central Committee held its meetings, important decisions, including the planning of terrorist acts, were taken, and correspondence was dealt with. All party documents and funds were kept under the personal surveillance of Natalia Poll. At the trial Bardovsky would not admit membership of 'Proletariat' or 'Narodnaya Volya'. But as registers of members of illegal organisations were not usually kept, formal evidence of membership was unimportant. On the other hand there can be no doubt that Bardovsky was personally involved in all the major questions concerning the strategy, tactics and activities of the Polish party for the eight or nine months between the arrest of the first group of the leadership and the second group in 1884, when Kunicki and Rechniewski were caught. Kunicki, who was staying in the judge's flat, was arrested there.

The close personal collaboration between the second set of leaders of 'Proletariat' and 'Narodnaya Volya' was best manifested in the Degayev affair, which reached its dramatic climax in the autumn of 1883, when one would have expected the Poles to be entirely immersed in rebuilding the leadership and party organisations, after the blows which 'Proletariat' had just suffered at the hands of the police. At this very moment the leader of the remnants of the Russian revolutionary organisation, Sergey Degayev, confessed to his comrades that while he had been sending them to assassinate high Tsarist officials, he had at the same time been denouncing them to the inspector of the secret police, Lieutenant-Colonel Grigory Sudeykin. Degayev agreed to kill Sudeykin as an act of penitence, and Kunicki, who was close to Degayev in the party's hierarchy, left Warsaw for St Petersburg where he organised the assassination of the police officer, and arranged, together with Tadeusz Rechniewski, another leader of 'Proletariat', Degayev's escape to the West.

In the meantime the police found out from some workers kept in the Citadel prison about Henryk Dulęba, the only man in the party's leadership in close contact with the workers. He was arrested on 13 January 1884, and with his disappearance the last Workers' Circle of the party in Warsaw melted away.

A few days later Kunicki appeared in Bardovsky's flat. The remaining members of the Central Committee decided to dispatch him to Paris and Geneva on an important mission.

The first task of the mission was concerned with providing the party with additional printed propaganda material. When Kunicki left Warsaw on 3 February 1884 the security situation of the party was rapidly deteriorating. The fourth issue of *Proletariat* had appeared with great difficulty in the second half of November. But it was becoming more and more difficult to assemble enough print in one place to set the next issue (the fifth issue appeared in May 1884). Kunicki therefore had to assemble a group of reliable persons living in the West and with their help renew the publication of the periodical *Przedświt* (*Dawn*). This was then to be smuggled, with the help of German Social Democrats, into the Kingdom. The second part of his mission, of greater historical importance, was to get in touch with the leadership of 'Narodnaya Volya', which was supposedly now established in the West, and at last realise the formal agreement between the Polish and Russian revolutionary socialists for a political and organisational unification of forces in the struggle against the Tsarist autocracy which had been so long desired. Since the Wilno conference (see pp. 75–8) this had been the goal of the leaders of 'Proletariat'. The arrests which hit the Polish party repeatedly after September 1883 were an additional spur to find strength from sources outside their own party. Kunicki, more than anyone else, knew how weak 'Narodnaya Volya' was at that moment. But his romantic inclinations and his poor judgment of political reality made him believe in a still glorious future for the Russian revolutionary terrorists. This conviction was evidently shared by the few who in the beginning of 1884 formed the Central Committee of the party. A document[14] which is dated 'Warsaw, February 1st, 1884', has as its main title: 'General principles of the programme and organisational activities of the Central Committee of the Social Revolutionary Party Proletariat.' The sub-heading was: 'Appeal to the Executive Committee of the Party "Narodnaya Volya".' It represents no doubt the views of the leadership of the party on all important matters of a political nature.

The *General Principles* started with the orthodox marxist statement that 'Proletariat' 'must base itself solely on the working class, which is here [in Poland] the only revolutionary element'. This was to a great extent also in accordance with the views of many of the Russians who were at that time disappointed with the failure of their fore-runners to win over the peasantry for the revolution. But while 'Narodnaya Volya' hoped to gain the support of the more liberal part of the Russian gentry, the Poles talked with contempt of the 'Szlachta' and the new urban middle classes, whom they described as 'our enemies not only of socialism but of any revolution'. The revolutionary party, continued the *General Principles*, was at present unable, because of the 'political conditions', to become a real mass movement. It could organise only those who were already socialists. But at the same time it had to propagate the 'class distinction' of the workers and thus prepare them to 'fight against the privileged classes and the government' for the workers' day-to-day needs and interests. Thus the situation of the workers might improve even before the victorious revolution. To achieve all their aims the revolutionary party had the 'most successful weapon in its hands: economic terror and its inseparable counterpart political terrorism, which appears in many forms'. The party wanted to pursue these tactics 'where the majority of the population speaks Polish'. The ultimate aim was to 'liquidate the present government and to take power into its [the Central Committee's, as is explained in the next sentence] own hands'. In the leading article in the Warsaw periodical *Proletariat* No. 3, 20 October 1883, written by Waryński, the term 'Dictatorship of the Proletariat' is used for the first time. The Polish party reserved to itself full independence in leading its 'economic activities', meaning the day-to-day struggle of the workers against their employers. But it stated that:

(1) the Polish proletariat can dislodge the Russian government only together with the revolutionary forces of the other parts of the Russian empire; (2) that these forces are assembled and organised under the banner of 'Narodnaya Volya'; (3) that this party, whose help in overthrowing the government is indispensable for the Polish proletariat, has decided on this goal so as to be able to carry on socialist reforms; (4) that the struggle against a despotic centralised government has to be correspondingly led and harmonised in all its manifestations over the whole territory which is under the common yoke; the Central Committee [of 'Proletariat'] takes part in this struggle in full agreement with the Executive Committee [of 'Narodnaya Volya'] as the representative of the Social Revolutionary Party active in the Russian state.

Having just declared themselves an organic part of the all-Russian revolutionary movement whose sole representative was 'Narodnaya Volya', the Poles logically deduced all the political consequences, stating that they would not join the revolution until they had received the password from the Russian party. But they significantly added in the same sentence that after the outbreak or victory of the revolution (this is left obscure – perhaps by design?) the Polish 'Central Committee will separate itself' from the Russians 'as an independent unit which in the sphere of its activities will carry out possible reforms depending upon local conditions'.

In conclusion, the document proposed that the Red Cross organisations of both parties, devoted to helping comrades and their families who had suffered because of their revolutionary activities, should work in unity and that both parties should not initiate agreement with any other group active in the respective regions without the assent of the party whose sphere of action it was.

Kunicki arrived in Paris in the first week of February 1884, and had detailed consultations with the Polish socialist emigrés who considered themselves members of 'Proletariat'. Together with one of them, Maria Jankowska (the wife of Stanisław Mendelson), he met the representatives of 'Narodnaya Volya', Lev Tikhomirov, Marya Oshanina-Olovienikova, German Lopatin and Galina Tshernyavskaya. We do not exactly know what went on during these talks, but there is circumstantial evidence that the representatives of 'Proletariat', no doubt under the influence of those who were living in the West and who could observe, and admire, the growing influence of socialist and trade union movements working within a democratic framework, expressed some doubts about terrorism as the only political weapon of revolutionaries. In the theoretical periodical of the Poles, published abroad,[15] they said at this time that terrorism 'must have . . . the support of social classes'; that 'terrorist action appears only in special conditions', and above all 'the party may recognise terror as a means, but cannot be a terrorist party'. In this way the Poles supported the unorthodox group of former members of the Russian party, the so-called 'Young Narodnaya Volya' who despaired of the terrorist activities, which were already more damaging to the cause of freedom in Russia than to the Tsarist government. What 'Proletariat' accepted fully was the right to use personal violence on traitors, police spies and also on the most obnoxious factory managers if, after proper warning had been given, they still did not mend their ways. As we shall see later, they used violence against the first two categories, sent a couple of warnings to the 'class enemy', but never carried out their threats against any hateful factory owner.

As a result of the talks between the representatives of both parties a document was signed, known as the 'Confidential Agreement of the Party "Proletariat" with the Party "Narodnaya Volya" '.[16]

It began by accepting the ideological document, dated 1 February 1884, as the basis for the Agreement. It then went on to spell out in detail the more important mechanics for its implementation. Of these, the most significant was the acknowledgment that the Executive Committee of the Russian party was the only one empowered to make any agreements relating to the whole country and the sole organiser of revolutionary activities in the armed forces. The activities of the Polish party were limited to the area of the Kingdom of Poland. The Russian Executive Committee was to have one of its members participating in the meetings of the Central Committee of 'Proletariat', and vice versa. In fact Kunicki, the leader of 'Proletariat' after the arrest of Waryński, was also the official representative of 'Narodnaya Volya' in the Poles' Central Committee. There could be no closer merging of leadership between the Polish and Russian revolutionaries. It never happened again.

This confidential agreement was solemnly ratified by the Executive Committee whose place of residence was given as St Petersburg. Actually, it was signed by the party's representation abroad. The Russian document was dated 1 March 1884 and was printed in the publications of both parties.[17] The Russians acknowledged that 'respecting the independence and the free development of every nation' and taking into account the 'different social conditions' existing between the Russians and Poles, there was no place for a 'complete identity of means' to be used by both parties. 'Because of this the full merger of the "Narodnaya Volya" party with the Polish party "Proletariat" could rather harm the activities of Russian and Polish socialists.' But at the same time 'the struggle of the Russian and Polish socialists cannot but be identical as far as the overthrowing of our common enemy, the Russian government, is concerned. In this case the moral unity of the Russian and Polish socialists can and must take the form of a formal union.' The Russians made it clear that they were the moving spirit of the revolution while the Poles 'join [them] as a supporting unit'.

Never before had popular political movements in Poland and Russia found enough common ground to ally their forces for an agreed goal. On the contrary, there had been cases in Polish history, especially on the eve of the last partition of Poland at the end of the eighteenth century, when selfish magnates (e.g. the Targowica Confederation in 1782) called on Russian help to crush what they believed to be radical reformist movements in their own nation. It is true that in the nineteenth century, after the collapse of the Napoleonic era, Prince Adam Czartoryski tried for a time to collaborate with the Russians in order to preserve as much freedom as possible for Congress Poland, which had been constituted by the Congress of Vienna in 1815 as an autonomous part of the Russian empire. And in the second half of that century another Polish nobleman, Alexander Wielopolski, also tried to collaborate with Alexander II. But each time the action was undertaken, not only without the support or even the acquiescence of the politically conscious parts of the nation, but against their most energetic opposition. The Confidential Agreement of 1884 between the first Polish socialist party and the Russian revolutionaries opened a new chapter in the nation's history. It signified a change of attitude in a section of Polish society towards at least one of the country's neighbours. From then on a part of the Polish Left no longer saw every Russian as an enemy of the Poles. They went further. They discovered among them comrades-in-arms, fighting in unity a common enemy. Most Polish marxists never discarded this tradition, and never gave up the hope of a Polish–Russian revolutionary alliance, not even when Joseph Visyarionovitch Stalin became the ruler of Russia, and did his best to exterminate them.

But in the conditions then prevailing in St Petersburg as well as in Warsaw, the Agreement remained a theoretical exercise. 'Narodnaya Volya' was dying a painful death, the Polish 'Proletariat' was soon to reach a crisis, and the shadows of its approaching collapse were already growing longer, although not yet recognised or anticipated by Kunicki and his romantic friends. Only a few active members of both organisations were still alive when, thirty years later, the Russian revolution arrived, and won.

While negotiating with the Russian revolutionaries, Kunicki at the same time consolidated the foreign base of the Warsaw leadership. We have seen (p. 79) that in May 1883, when Waryński visited the Polish socialist colony in Geneva, he was unable to win over the majority of the editorial board of the periodical *Przedświt* to his point of view that the Polish labour movement should stay divided, within the framework of the divided country. The majority of the board considered the socialist groups and organisations then emerging in the Russian Kingdom of Poland, in Austro-Hungarian Galicia, and in the German provinces of Poznań, Pomerania and Silesia as parts of one body: Polish society. Waryński rejected this attitude as nationalistic and as contradicting marxist doctrine on the decisive role of class division and class struggle in determining the politics of socialists. Kunicki, coming to Paris and Geneva nine months later, found the situation radically changed. Two of the more nationalistically-inclined members of the editorial board, Kazimierz Dłuski and Witold Piekarski, had left it a few months earlier. Szymon Dikstein had changed his opinions. Stanisław Mendelson and Cezaryna Wojnarowska had joined the board after being released from prisons in Berlin and Cracow respectively, after having served a few months each for prohibited socialist propaganda.[18]

Kunicki found every one of them ready to accept in its entirety the ideological platform of the Warsaw 'Proletariat'. As they said in their declaration introducing the new publications which they planned to issue:[19]

A periodical published abroad, and which defends a strictly defined pro-gramme must base itself on the native organisation; if it wants to have any influence it must represent this [native] organisation *vis-à-vis* other socialist parties. Such a socialist organisation, conscious of its aims, with a precise programme is Proletariat which has existed in the Kingdom of Poland for the last two years.

Thus 'Proletariat' for a time controlled all Polish socialist publications produced either in the Kingdom or abroad. A firm calling itself 'Walka Klas' ('Class Struggle') was formed, which immediately proceeded to republish *Przedświt*, which was devoted to discussions and observations of a more intellectual nature, and also *Walka Klas*, written in more popular language for the mass of workers. Stanisław Mendelson became the editor of both period-icals, being the leader, even the 'dictator', of the emigré group of

I

Polish socialists. He was a most talented publicist; witty, quick in politics, full of ideas, often very unconventional. 'Not satisfied with any ready-made doctrine, not bound by any theoretical prejudices, always restless, courageous and ruthless.'[20] After the collapse of the mass party in its native land he considered himself and his group abroad as its leaders and representatives. Less than a decade later he broke the anti-national tradition of the early Polish marxists and made *Przedświt* the mouthpiece of the newly formed and patriotically-inclined Polish Socialist Party (PPS).

Although formally the party was the same as that which, under Ludwik Waryński, had formulated its principles in the Programme of 1 September 1882 (pp. 58–67), under Stanisław Kunicki it moved, in its propaganda, and even more in its actions, nearer to the terrorist practice of the original 'Narodnaya Volya'. A marxist historian of 'Proletariat', otherwise very sympathetic to its principles and leaders, wrote of this change which came with the Kunicki leadership:[21] 'Terror, apparently almighty, based on individual heroism was permitted to mask the real weakness of the movement. Terror satisfied the need for action, the exalted urge for sacrifice, the vivid imagination, the impatience of proselytes. Especially the young were deeply impressed by it, dazzled and carried away.'

But like all meteors it passed away as quickly as it appeared.

THE CURTAIN FALLS

In March 1884 Stanisław Kunicki was provided by his Russian friends with a false passport in the name of Dragolub Diuritz, a Serbian student allegedly studying at Heidelberg, and he returned to Warsaw. Even he could not pretend to himself that an all-Russian revolution, organised and led by 'Narodnaya Volya', had the slightest hope of immediate success. On the contrary, it was the organisation of the revolutionaries themselves which lay in ruins.

He found the situation of his 'Proletariat' party only slightly better. The gendarmerie evidently knew enough to direct its heavy blows more and more often against the most active members of the party. In the spring of 1884 there were more leading comrades behind the walls of the Tenth Pavilion prison of the Warsaw Citadel than outside. Kunicki was seized by one thought: the need to liquidate all those who were suspected of betraying the party from within to the authorities, and by physically attacking police spies to frighten off any future aspirants for this occupation. He was one of those who believed that 'We do not need the masses for this kind of struggle: such a fight must be the result of individual action, and [must] take the form of concealed, secret punishment and vengeance.'22

The workers' mass base of the party, built up with so much thought, inventiveness and sacrifice by Waryński and his closest collaborators in 1882–3, was destroyed by the police. On the eve of Kunicki's return from abroad, during the night of the 1st and the early hours of the 2nd of March, the police encircled the whole of the working-class district of Warsaw, and searched the flats, albeit with only slight results, though some copies of the party periodical were found. A few workers were put in prison. No wonder that people were fearful of joining this dangerous underground organisation. Kunicki and Dębski, the only members of the Central Committee of 'Proletariat' still free, used this state of fear to mobilise what was left of the party organisation for individual terrorism, the last weapon of those in despair. In an article which Dębski wrote for the sixth, unpublished, issue of *Proletariat*, and which survived only in the police archives,23 he said in connection with the assassination of Sudeykin by Degayev: 'All citizens of the Russian empire came to the conclusion that the struggle against the government can give desired results only with the help of terror, which establishes the sole counterpoise to the tsarist despotism.'

The only organisation Kunicki formed during his party leadership was therefore the Fighting Squad, of which he was the commander-in-chief and which consisted of eight men, most of whom were very courageous indeed. One of the eight was an exception: the young sculptor Edmund Baranowski was a police spy.24 Kunicki, alas, trusted him more than any other member of the squad. In many cases Baranowksi laid the plans for terrorist acts, and naturally kept his police chiefs informed of their smallest details. Thus from beginning to end the terrorist organisation of 'Proletariat' was controlled, and, indeed, led by the police intelligence bureau under the supervision of Lieutenant-Colonel Tcherkasov and Major, later Lieutenant-Colonel, Sekerzhinsky.

It was at their instigation that Baranowski suggested to Kunicki that they should widen the terrorist front and include in their targets not only the personally insignificant police spies known to the party, but also high political officials like the major himself and the assistant-procurator, Yankulyo. He also suggested the destruction by explosives of the procurator's office in Warsaw where all the records concerning the party and its already arrested leaders were kept. Needless to say, the designated victims of the attacks were completely safe. They were not only ready to pounce on the perpetrators early enough to forestall the attack, but made themselves even safer through Baranowski, who had to oversee the preparation of the explosives and who made sure they were all but harmless (a piece of dynamite did explode in the laboratory of the conspirators but even then nobody suffered seriously). Yet the very fact of forming a special organisation to commit acts of personal violence on state and police officials made easier the task of those in the political administration who wanted to suppress the first mass movement of Polish socialists both as a subversive and as an organisation of revolutionary terrorists, to whom para. 249 of the Tsarist criminal code could be applied. There could be only one punishment in such case: death on the gallows. The excitable Kunicki fell into the trap prepared by the gendarmerie. He also paid the full price for his imprudence.

It would be unfair to blame only Kunicki, or Dębski, or the agent-provocateurs whom the gendarmerie planted among the revolutionary socialists for the sharp turning to terrorism from mass propaganda, which had characterised the previous period (1882–3) of 'Proletariat's' activities. At this time the economy of the Kingdom suffered from an acute crisis, which resulted in mass unemployment in the towns and cities. The new entrepreneurs were not there for charity. They cut their labour force according to market conditions. There were no public funds to help the unemployed and their families. No trade union, or other defence organisation of the workers was allowed to function. Extreme poverty engulfed the workers' quarters in Łódź and Warsaw, in Żyrardów and Zgierz. Misery and helplessness were the soil in which the idea that a desperate act by a lonely man, armed with a knife or a revolver, could challenge the government and overthrow the whole system of capitalist exploitation, could strike root, and attract many of the unemployed. That hungry people turned, as so many had done in the past, to the idea of a liberating Messiah or a romantic Robin Hood, should surprise no-one. That a party, led by intellectually trained people, who believed themselves to belong to the vanguard of rational Man and who maintained that they had discovered the immutable laws governing human history, should have deceived themselves, and others, so far as to think that a fighting squad of eight men, who did not know how to produce a decent bomb, and for whom a revolver or stiletto were the highest form of personal ammunition, would shatter the existing order, was worse than folly. The wonder is that they really believed in it.

One milder form of psychological terror were threats addressed to factory owners, managers and foremen. Once they achieved their aim. Ignacy Poznański, the founder of the very large textile combine in Łódź, forced his employees, good Roman Catholics, to work on Church holidays. On 25 February 1884, the Workers' Committee of the local 'Proletariat' organisation sent him a letter, telling him that if he again sacked people who refused to work on holidays, as had happened on 8 February, the day of the Virgin of Gromnica, he would be 'severely punished'. According to the report in the underground press the threat 'was successful'.[25] But this was not always so. A more stubborn entrepreneur simply ignored the threats. The secret organisation was in fact unable to mete out the 'punishment' they had threatened and no 'capitalist' personally suffered any harm at the hands of 'Proletariat'.

It was different when it came to terrorism against police spies and their own comrades who had become active collaborators of the gendarmerie. In all tribal history a traitor is much more contemptible than an oppressor, who is generally alien by race, religion, nationality or class. A traitor is a part of one's own social structure. He does not act in the name of an alien law, but breaks the rules of the group to which he himself belongs. He is a criminal to those who suffer because of his deeds or behaviour. While many radicals or socialists in the nineteenth century rejected terrorism as a political weapon, they were much more ambivalent on the question of 'punishing' traitors. This is certainly true of the socialist movements in eastern and southern Europe where governments were authoritarian, and used agent-provocateurs to catch active socialists, and then locked them up in prisons often for innocuous activities.

Soon after Kunicki's return to Warsaw a second attempt was made on 26 March, in Zgierz, to kill the police collaborator, Śremski. Armed with a stiletto, two members of the local party organisation, Stanisław Bugajski and Kazimierz Tomaszewski, textile workers, attacked him, again wounding him only slightly.[26] Civilians helped the police to catch the 20-year-old Bugajski red-handed. During the police interrogation he disclosed the name of his collaborator in the assassination. Tomaszewski, after hiding for two months, gave himself up to the gendarmerie. For the first time in the history of 'Proletariat' Article 249 of the Criminal Code, which provided for hanging as the penalty, was used in the charge in this case. Since then it became the sword of Damocles hanging over the heads of many of 'Proletariat's' active members and of all its leaders.

Yet Kunicki, who was at this moment the only active member of the Central Committee of 'Proletariat', was obsessed with the idea of fighting the system by liquidating police spies. The fifth issue of the Warsaw periodical, dated 1 May 1884, had a list of eight names of alleged police informers and spies. Kunicki immediately decided to organise the assassination of two of them. One was the leader of the party in Zgierz, Franciszer Helszer, a textile worker. The other was a certain Michał Skrzypczyński, a bus conductor and a member of the Warsaw party organisation.

Helszer had at first been delegated to kill Śremski. But he had hesitated. Pacanowksi, the Central Committee's 'agent' in nearby Łódź, himself an excitable young man, readily accepted as proven the suspicion that Helszer did not keep his promises because he was himself a police agent. Without much ado Kunicki wrote out a death sentence on Helszer, signed and sealed in the name of the Central Committee, and gave it to Pacanowski to be immediately executed. He also handed over to him a revolver, a stiletto and a drug to be put into Helszer's cigarettes. On the same day, on 28 May, Kunicki signed a death sentence on Skrzypczyński.

On 6 June the 20-year-old Jan Pietrusiński shot Helszer in the head while he was smoking a drugged cigarette offered to him by another of his comrades, Teofil Bloch. Helszer died two days later without regaining consciousness. Nobody was arrested on the spot. Technically it was the most successful act of terror committed by members of 'Proletariat'. Alas, the victim was an innocent man, and a loyal comrade to his murderers.[27] Shortly afterwards Pietrusiński and Bloch were apprehended by the police.

For the first time none of the conspirators was caught on the scene of the assassination. Kunicki and his friends in the Warsaw leadership were delighted. They decided at once to publish a leaflet (also in German for the German-speaking workers in Łódź and its surrounding district, where many were active members of 'Proletariat'), in which they repeated the unwarranted accusation against Helszer and ended with the words: 'Then let everybody remember, that he who for any reason will betray [us] because of fear or for personal gain, as a free man or in prison, can expect certain death.' The leaflet was signed by the Central Committee.[28]

The threat of death for betrayal while in prison was founded on depressing information reaching the leadership of what was happening inside the cells of the Warsaw Citadel. The police net was tightening ominously. In June the gendarmes arrested a 20-year-old student, Feliks Kon, who was then one of the most prominent party members and especially active in the secret printing press.

Nothing could stop Kunicki. Through Bardovsky he came into

close contact with a group of revolutionary Russian officers in the Warsaw garrison (Lury, Ingelstrom, Sokolsky and a few others). Kunicki wanted them to consider 'Proletariat' rather than 'Narodnaya Volya' as their political home. This they refused to do. They would help the Poles with money (especially Captain Lury, who could, and did, use government funds of which he was in charge to support 'Proletariat's' meagre treasury). They sometimes hid illegal literature in their official apartments. But they declined to take orders from Kunicki, who expected them to start a propaganda campaign in their units with the aim of building up a large revolutionary organisation among officers and privates. The officers thought such plans premature, and therefore extremely dangerous.

Kunicki then persuaded the Russian Judge Bardovsky to write a manifesto[29] to officers, which he planned to send by post to all those in the garrisons in the Kingdom of Poland who were known for their progressive opinions. The manifesto described the Tsar's régime in most sarcastic terms, called on the military to rebel against the system because 'only the social revolution will deliver Russia from the evil which strangles her' and expected the officers to form revolutionary circles to collaborate with the Polish 'Proletariat', which, as the leaflet said, was closely allied with 'Narodnaya Volya'.

But before the manifesto could be despatched, the gendarmerie struck. Through informers, of whom a member of the Fighting Squad, Edmund Baranowski, was in this case the most successful,[30] it was not difficult to discover the place which became, not only the meeting and living place of the party's leaders, but also its address for correspondence and even for part of the underground printing shop. On 1 July 1884 Lieutenant Tcherkasov, at the head of a large detachment of gendarmes, burst into Bardovsky's flat. The operation was so swift that nothing had been destroyed. The police found the archives of 'Proletariat', the official party stamp and also those of the 'agenture' of 'Narodnaya Volya'. Among the correspondence kept in the flat the gendarmes found letters written by Waryński and Alexandra Jentys, which only a day before had been smuggled out from the

Tenth Pavilion of the Citadel. Also among the police haul was Russian type used for underground revolutionary publications, and the manuscript of the manifesto to the officers written by Bardovsky. This made him a major criminal in the eyes of the authorities. Kunicki was arrested, together with Bardovsky and Natalia Poll, but maintained that everything illegal found in the flat was his. It helped nobody.

On the basis of the letters and lists the police picked up most of the party's group of students at the veterinary school. Two members of the leadership, Ludwik Janowicz and Alexander Dębski, were at that moment away from Warsaw. They immediately returned and found that one party cell, the Fighting Squad, was still left intact. Of course, they did not know or suspect that this was the result of a decision of the secret police department, which through Baranowski was able to control its activities and at the same time use it as a source of information about the further plans of those revolutionaries who had escaped exposure and arrest. The two leaders and the members of the Squad worked out a list of nearly a dozen men whom they considered responsible for the latest arrests, and began preparations for a whole series of assassinations. Three revolvers and a few stilettos were acquired – not much of an arsenal to serve against so many.

A few days later, on 30 July, a police agent and former member of socialist groups, a certain Huzarski, recognised the few remaining leaders in a café, where they had met to complete their plans for the next assassinations. He called the police and a struggle followed. Two, Dębski and Sławiński, succeeded in escaping during the mêlée. Janowicz determined not to let himself be arrested (he had incriminating documents on him), drew his revolver and twice shot at Huzarski, wounding him (and, accidentally, himself) only slightly. He was arrested and taken to prison.

Dębski and Sławiński had no alternative but to flee abroad. Not one of the party leadership was left to control and lead the Fighting Squad. Its members were still ready to go ahead with their plans against individual agents of the police. Unfortunately for Skrzypczyński, the bus conductor and police informer,[31] when it was decided to kill him Baranowski, the agent-provocateur was not present at the meeting. On 7 August, Michał Ossowski, a 21-year-old shoemaker, struck the spy with a stiletto with such force that he died a few days later. A fortnight later, Ossowski was arrested in Łódź, denounced by another spy inside the party organisation.

Frightened by the assault on Skrzypczyński, the authorities decided to end their game with Baranowski's Fighting Squad. Arrests followed. The Squad was no more.

Before Dębski escaped to the West he handed over all the party documents he held to a 19-year-old teacher, Maria Bohuszewicz. She came from a family with long patriotic traditions, and was the maternal granddaughter of the nation's hero, Tadeusz Kościuszko.[32] At this time she had not become directly involved in the political work of the party. Together with Feliks Kon's bride, Rozalia Felsenhardt, she was immersed in the activities of the party's Red Cross, which was desperately short of means to help the many comrades in prisons and their families, especially of the working-class members, who had lost their only breadwinners. Bohuszewicz and Felsenhardt now formed the nucleus of a new Central Committee. With courage and energy less than a dozen people led by these two young women started to rebuild some semblance of an underground organisation. They had practically no funds. Contacts with the party colonies in Geneva and Paris were non-existent. The party organisations outside Warsaw had also been destroyed by arrests and by the resulting panic among the members.

One of the first problems discussed by this new, third leadership group of 'Proletariat' was their attitude towards the use of terrorism. The two women had a much better understanding of existing conditions, and were much more practical, although no less courageous, than Kunicki, the former party leader. They both did their utmost to curb the more reckless members of the new nucleus. What they approved of was economic terrorism, and once Bohuszewicz posted a threatening note to a factory owner, a certain Żerański, telling him that if he did not change his 'inhuman treatment of his workers' the Central Committee of 'Proletariat' would have to consent to the demand of the local committee to execute him.[33] As was discovered later, one of those in the leadership who most vigorously propagated the idea of terrorism on the widest front was Piotr Piński vel Piotrowski, who was an agent-provocateur, acting on the orders of the secret police.

Maria Bohuszewicz and her colleagues concentrated on producing propaganda material after the gendarmerie had seized the large stock of political literature in Bardovsky's apartment and during subsequent searches and arrests. They had contacts neither with the West nor with the Russian revolutionaries, whose organisation, 'Narodnaya Volya', had practically ceased to function. The 'Proletariat' printing shop was destroyed by the party workers themselves after the arrests in July and August. The new leadership had only a primitive hectograph at their disposal.

The last months of 1884 were devoted to two tasks. One was to rebuild the broken contacts with workers in the larger Warsaw factories, and to re-establish organisations in the provinces. The other was to find means by which the party's Red Cross could help the many arrested comrades, more than a hundred at this time, who had no-one to look after them.

To a great extent both aims were achieved. Loose contacts were established with big factories, and small rank and file organisations were formed, consisting mostly of artisans (shoemakers) and apprentices. Unexpectedly there was also a strong and practical response in the textile centres, in Łódź, Zgierz and Tomaszów Mazowiecki.

One member of the new leadership, an unemployed locksmith, Władyslaw Wilczyński, then fell under the influence of a Serb cabinet-maker, Andra Bankovic, an experienced socialist, who had come to Warsaw in search of revolutionary activity.[34] Bankovic knew and admired the tactics of the Western labour movement. He consequently persuaded Wilczyński, who was very popular with the unemployed, to organise a demonstration in the centre of Warsaw, and thus draw the attention of the authorities and of society at large to their miserable life. At meetings of workers, with the participation of Wilczyński and other speakers from 'Proletariat', it was decided to demonstrate on 2 March 1885. Two hundred unemployed workers assembled on that day. In accordance with the decision of the party's Central Committee no member of the intelligentsia was supposed to take part. Wilczyński and Bankovic led the marchers through the very centre of Warsaw. The police looked with tolerance on the workers who were only asking for employment. At one moment Bankovic made a speech to the demonstrators suggesting that they should march to the castle, the residence of General Hurko, the Governor-General. And so they did. Once there they were surrounded by a strong force of police. Bankovic addressed himself to the police chief in broken French, asking for work for the unemployed. The response of the police to this most peaceful gathering was to arrest 146 of the demonstrators. They were all soon released, with the exception of Bankovic who was transferred to the Tenth Pavilion.

The demonstration of workers, the first of its kind in Warsaw, made a very great impression on all classes of Polish society. The Central Committee assembled a few hours later and decided to publish a leaflet about it. Two party members, of whom one was a printer's apprentice, quickly prepared a thousand copies, dated 4 March 1885, a real achievement even for a stronger and richer organisation than 'Proletariat' then was. The leaflet[35] blamed the economic system which punished the workers with unemployment and hunger for 'producing too much'. It then criticised the decision of the authorities to send for 'cossacks and gendarmes' to arrest peacefully demonstrating workers and asked them to draw the conclusion that the government was 'openly taking sides with our capitalist oppressors'. It called on the workers to defend their human dignity and organise 'under the slogan Liberty, Factories and Farms'.

The mass arrests in the autumn of 1883 (of the Waryński leadership) and in the summer of 1884 (the Kunicki group) considerably reduced the number of people in the party who were marxist-inclined. Among the third leadership group under Maria

Bohuszewicz we find only one person, Leon Winiarski, a 21-year-old student of Warsaw University, who probably with the help of his brother Wolf, also a member of 'Proletariat', tried to keep up the tradition of spreading marxist ideas among the first Polish socialists. He was the author of two pamphlets of this kind. One was called 'About crises and their sources', and the other 'On supplementary values', being a popularisation of the first volume of Karl Marx's *Das Kapital*. They were hectographed by party members and distributed among workers in public places.

But this strictly marxist attitude to politics was by then no longer the only or even the prevailing line pursued by the party. On 10 June 1885 the Central Committee of the party published another hectographed manifesto to the peasants.[36] Its title was quite new in 'Proletariat's' literature: 'In the name of the Faith and Freedom.' It was quite obvious that the faith was not that of Karl Marx but of God and His Son. The manifesto, after characterising the exploitation of the village population, called on the peasants in the name of 'God who created us and ordered for us the same laws' to fight against the injustices created by evil men. The party called on the peasants to unite 'in the name of the Redeemer, who died on the cross, the Christ who suffered so much pain' and to 'give an oath in God's presence' to fight for the sake of themselves, their wives and children.

That the appeal to traditional and deeply felt Christian symbols and emotions was likely to receive a more eager response from Polish peasants or workers than the explanation of Hegelian dialectics and Ricardo's theory of labour values there can be no doubt whatsoever. The most prominent party agitator in Łódź and its district, Wojciech Sławiński, a cabinet-maker, always talked of 'Jesus Christ who established the social-revolutionary cause'. He even taught his listeners revolutionary songs using the melodies of traditional church hymns. The party members in neighbouring Zgierz on 26 May 1885 put up on a main road a large white wooden cross, with an iron body of Christ, round which a hundred workers assembled and intoned revolutionary songs.[37]

To collect funds for those in prison, the party organised evening dances and balls. To give work to unemployed comrades the party founded two co-operatives, one producing furniture and the other for bookbinding; the latter naturally was also used for producing the party's pamphlets. Bohuszewicz and most of her collaborators saw in the co-operative movement a way of helping the unemployed in general, a 'reformist' act which would have been severely condemned by Kunicki or even Waryński.*

The police had not only Piński in the ranks of the party. They knew from their agents about every movement made by Bohuszewicz and her friends, who were amateurs in the art of conspiracy. There were plans in the party to produce a new, the sixth, issue of the party periodical, to publish a manifesto to the intelligentsia (which Kon wrote in his prison cell and smuggled out with the help of Rozalia Felsenhardt), and even to start a satirical journal. And, of course, hot-heads, incited by Piński, the agent-provocateur and a member of the Central Committee, still vaguely talked of new acts of terrorism. The chief of the gendarmerie, Lieutenant-Colonel Sekerzhinsky, decided to wait no longer. He was probably also afraid that he might lose the control over their activities which he maintained through Piński and at least three more of his agents working in the organisation, because he received information that two important representatives of the emigré groups working in Geneva and Paris had arrived in Warsaw. They were Alexander Dębski and Stefan Ulrych, both men of considerable experience as political conspirators.[38] They also brought with them a large number of issues of the periodical *Walka Klas*.

In the early hours of 30 September the searches and arrests began. Maria Bohuszewicz, Rozalia Felsenhardt, both the brothers Winiarski, and thirty-two other active members of the Warsaw organisation of the party were sent into the prison cells of the Tenth Pavilion of the Citadel. Unfortunately, Bohuszewicz had kept in her room the party correspondence, the lists of members and contacts outside Warsaw too. More arrests followed

---

* It is therefore no surprise that the communist historian of 'Proletariat', L. Baumgarten, disapproves of the first socialist co-operatives in Poland.

as far away as Kowno. Soon the party organisation in Łódź, Zgierz and Tomaszów were smashed, thanks to police agent Piński. Altogether sixty persons were sent to prison in Warsaw and the provinces accused of belonging to the party.[39]

The action of the police in the autumn of 1885 virtually liquidated the leadership and organisational base of 'Proletariat'. But not completely.

7 THE GOVERNMENT'S REVENGE

THE LAST ACT

All in all the procurator's office in Warsaw prepared cases against 190 persons of both sexes and of all ages between 17 and 60 who were accused of belonging to the Polish Social Revolutionary Party 'Proletariat' in the years 1883 and 1884.[1] In the next two years another seventy people were added to this list. The material situation of the imprisoned, and that of their families, was often desperate. There was nobody, after the arrest in September 1885 of Maria Bohuszewicz, Rozalia Felsenhardt and their collaborators in the clandestine Red Cross, to provide funds to help them. No aid could be expected from their Russian allies. 'Narodnaya Volya' was by then practically non-existent. The only hope lay in the Western Social Democratic parties. Stanisław Mendelson, who together with his wife Maria (Jankowska) established friendly personal relations with the prominent German Social Democratic leader and member of the Reichstag, the former naval officer Georg von Vollman, in a letter to him dated Paris, 17 October 1885, described the situation of the party at home thus:[2]

Our present situation is very difficult and very sad. Everywhere mass arrests, great misery in the prisons. We have until now 150 sentences (half to Siberia) – and now 100 arrests again. On top of it came personal tragedies – which also harm the party. We want to overcome the present difficulties, to restore courage to those who survived [in freedom], and to help the distressed. We have decided with Maria to write to you to ask you to act as an intermediatory between us and those comrades who would like to assist our cause and our co-fighters. I am sending to you ten subscription sheets, which you may be able to hand over to Swedish, Danish and German comrades.

The letter ends with Mendelson's address in Paris to which the collected money should be transmitted.

No wonder that Mendelson was in a state of near despair. Although the leaders of 'Proletariat' were in the well-guarded prison of the Warsaw Citadel, much of what happened there became known to their families, and to those few of their political friends who escaped the arrests in the autumn of 1883, in July 1884 and in September 1885. It was very depressing news indeed.

The mass arrests in the summer of 1884 put into the hands of the authorities many people who either could not for long withstand their more sophisticated interrogators or whose nerves were too weak to face real danger, or who were moral cowards, ready to betray their friends to save themselves from the severe consequences of their activities. Unfortunately too many knew too much.

The man who betrayed most, and knew almost everything, was Stanisław Pacanowski. He had been Kunicki's right-hand man, who had considered him his heir apparent in the party and to whom he personally handed over death sentences and the weapons with which to execute them. Pacanowski started collaborating with the prosecuting office only a month after his arrest. He apparently hoped to save himself from the consequences of personally organising the assassination of Helszer.

He was not the only one who helped the gendarmerie to uncover everything the party had done and planned to do, from the moment it was formed. Some of those who confessed (Pacanowski, Handelsman, Płoski, Zagórski, Gładysz) belonged to the intelligentsia. Many workers who confessed to everything they knew were partly or completely illiterate and at least in some cases signed documents which they did not fully understand (the additional difficulty was the fact that alleged statements were written in Russian, which Polish workers did not know).[3] They were also under tremendous pressure from their wives and children who were allowed to visit them during the interrogation period and who were living evidence of the material catastrophe which the arrests of the bread-winners had brought upon their families.

Although no physical tortures were used, the condition of complete isolation was more than some of the arrested could bear. Natalia Poll, full of remorse that mainly because of her Piotr Bardovsky's flat had become the headquarters of 'Proletariat', suffered a nervous breakdown during which she informed fully on all the activities of her husband, his officer friends, and

K

the Polish leaders for whom she cared and whom she had helped so much.

A special case was that of Stanisław Kunicki himself. At first he, like Waryński, Alexandra Jentys, Dulęba and many others, refused to admit anything, or to try to explain away his actions and opinions. But five weeks after his arrest the chief gendarmes and interrogating judges presented him with Pacanowski's signed statement that 'he [Kunicki] directed everything without any control and he had only a few assistants . . . but they were inexperienced people'. It was the same Pacanowksi who disclosed all the details of the murder of Helszer as ordered by Kunicki.[4] Two other members of the party told how Kunicki had organised the assault on Skrzypczyński. Thus he was made the instigator of all terrorist acts committed by the party, of which two had resulted in the death of the victims. He was also under constant moral pressure from his family, who wanted to save him from the gallows. On 1 October 1884 Kunicki wrote a letter to Byelanovsky, the chief of gendarmerie, in which he expressed his wish to serve the Tsarist secret police from then on and to disclose everything he knew about the party as the price of regaining his freedom.

He did not stop there. On 12 December he dictated to Byelanovsky, and then signed, a document of 53 pages,[5] which consisted of a full description of the two organisations in which he had held leading positions: the Russian 'Narodnaya Volya' and the Polish 'Proletariat'. He described the role played by some who were in prison still awaiting trial. He designated the role of Natalia Poll and Bardovsky as being of special significance.

Eleven days later in a letter to the same gendarme officer, who was the chief investigator of the 'Proletariat' case, Kunicki withdrew his confessions. He explained his previous decision to offer his services to the secret police and the information he had already given, as the result of shock at discovering that others had betrayed him and the party. He said further in this letter that he had then decided to win his freedom, and once abroad to make public the 'whole comedy' and thus 'make it impossible to persecute the people whom I vilified'.

With this last letter Kunicki made sure of his martyrdom. Yet by his previous confessions in all probability he brought about the execution of 20-year-old Jan Pietrusiński, Helszer's assassin. What, apart from a momentary lack of nerve, made him offer himself to the Tsarist police as a collaborator? It was, one can only assume, a diseased version of what is known among romantic Poles as Wallenrodism. It was an idea of the poet Adam Mickiewicz which influenced, and still impresses, young Poles when the physical power of their country's oppressors is too great to be overcome by a frontal assault. The hero of one of Mickiewicz's long poems, a leader of the Lithuanians oppressed and subjugated by the stronger Prussians, joined the fighting order of the grasping Knights of the Cross as the supposed German Konrad Wallenrod and led them treacherously into catastrophic defeat on the battlefield, thus annihilating the enemies of his people. Kunicki, unbalanced, romantic, no doubt influenced also by the nihilist ideas of 'revolutionary morality' fashionable at this time among some radical Russian groups, for a short moment trod the slippery path of deceit, which had destroyed more than one revolutionary in Russia and elsewhere. He did so without taking advice from any of his numerous political friends who were with him in the cells of the Warsaw Citadel. He withdrew, as we have seen, soon after regaining his balance of mind. From then on, during interrogations, at the trial, and on the gallows he behaved with great courage and determination.

It soon became clear to everyone, to the arrested, and to those outside the prison walls, that the threat of execution was now a real possibility, first for those who took a direct part in the three assassinations, and second for every leader of 'Proletariat' against whom it could be proved that he had taken the fatal decisions, helped to organise the assaults or had provided the assassins with their weapons. All the facts were in the files of the gendarmes and the state prosecutor.

The Bohuszewicz leadership of the party made plans to engineer the escape of the most endangered prisoners from the Citadel.

In July and August 1885 the organisation smuggled a few

small files into the prison to cut the iron bars of the cells. Nothing came of this. More serious was the attempt undertaken by Michał Woynicz, a member of 'Proletariat', who brought into the conspiracy the easy-going brother of one of the arrested, Antoni Janowicz. He was a class-mate in the officers' school of a Russian Second Lieutenant, Piotr Fursa, with whom, along with other officers of the gendarmerie and high officials, he spent his time, and money, playing cards. Fursa was the governor of the Tenth Pavilion, the prison in the Citadel. Through Janowicz, Woynicz became one of the card-playing group which often met inside the Citadel. He was thus able to find out the exact location of the prison cells, corridors and exits. In a letter dated 26 April 1947, written in New York where she then was living, the widow of Michał Woynicz, the English novelist Ethel Lillian Boole-Woynicz, recounted this episode in the life of her husband as follows:[6]

When it became evident that Bardowski, and Kunicki were likely to be executed, the Polish 'Proletariat' group decided to attempt a rescue. The success of their scheme, which included tunnel, rope-ladder, boat, and other elaborate preparations, depended on accurate timing by means of a signal to be given from the ramparts of the Citadel to the watchers below the cliffs. The signaller must have access to the ramparts during the night, and must therefore know the passwords. The 'Proletariat' applied to the Russian 'Narodnaya Volia' to lend a volunteer who could win the confidence of the gendarmerie officers in charge and obtain the passwords. My husband, Wilfred Michael Voynich (Wojnicz in Polish; born Kovno 1865; died New York 1930), then a student at Moscow University, had joined the 'Narodnaya Volia'. The assignment was offered to him because, in addition to certain other qualifications, he was a stranger to Warsaw and its police, and spoke Russian without any Polish accent. (Though a Pole, he had grown up in Lithuania, where Polish culture was suppressed and all education compulsorily russified.) Accordingly, provided with Russian passport and introductions, and with money to squander, he went to Warsaw, frequented the nightly card parties in the officers' quarters of the Citadel, and quickly won the favour of Lieut. Col. Bielanowski of the gendarmerie.

At that time the position of the gendarme officers in Warsaw was one of painful isolation. Polish society pointedly ignored their existence, only the most abandoned women would speak to them voluntarily, and even their own Russian colleagues of the regular army were sometimes but officially polite. Bielanowski in particular, a renegade Pole of bad reputation, ambitious and disappointed, found himself socially a leper. He was delighted to welcome a young man who lost money gracefully at cards and who sniggered over his anecdotes of how to obtain useful information from unwilling witnesses. In time, to save the trouble of escorting him to the gates in the small hours, my husband was given the passwords.

The preparations were almost completed when a vague hint from a traitor in another branch led to a search and to the discovery of the tunnel. Investigations and arrests followed; Bardowski, Kunicki, and two others were hanged, and Bielanowski revenged himself by compelling my husband to witness the execution and telling his mother that he had been shot.

The traitor who informed the authorities about the escape plan was Piński, in whom Maria Bohuszewicz confided all the details of the preparations for the escape, and who undertook to provide the escapees with places to hide in before they could be smuggled out of the country. Michał Woynicz, who, unknown to his wife, was an active member of 'Proletariat' (he said as much to Byelanovsky after his arrest) was exiled without trial for five years to eastern Siberia whence he later escaped to England.

At the beginning of January 1885 the police closed the files of the 190 members of 'Proletariat' arrested in 1883 and 1884. After a lengthy correspondence between the state prosecutor's office in Warsaw and the Imperial Ministry of Justice in St Petersburg the decision was taken to put on trial before a military tribunal in Warsaw twenty-nine persons who could be accused of organising and performing acts of terrorism, according to the dreaded para. 249 of the criminal code. Most of those who had betrayed their comrades, whose confessions were confirmed during the investigations, and whose role in the underground party was confined to attending clandestine meetings and reading forbidden tracts, were released from prison, some with only an admonition and others with the obligation to report periodically to the police.

Twenty-four others were administratively exiled to eastern Siberia for periods between three and five years. For some this was a sentence of slow death in a cruel, God-forsaken land. More than a hundred received prison sentences of between 2 and 16 months each.

On 23 November 1885 in a small hall in the Citadel the trial of the twenty-nine men accused of belonging to an illegal organisation, the Social Revolutionary Party 'Proletariat', began. Of their number, twenty-five were Poles. Judge Bardovsky, the officers Nicolai Lury, Andrey Ingelstrom and Zakhary Sokolsky were Russians. Although none of them was involved in the preparation or planning of terrorist acts, the Russian authorities, and the Tsar personally, were determined that their punishment for helping Polish revolutionaries should be harsher than that inflicted on the others and thus exemplary. The court consisted of two professional military judges, three colonels and two lieutenant-colonels in active service.

The accused were allowed to employ defence counsel, among whom there were first-class advocates, Poles and Russians. The presiding judge, General Vladimir Friderix, tried to observe the prescribed judicial procedure for a court. He let the accused say what they wanted and did not unnecessarily obstruct the defence even when it tried to show the irregular methods used by the police and the prosecutor's officials to make illiterate persons sign documents which were afterwards used against the accused.

Some of the accused, among them all four Russians, from the beginning of the trial denied the accusation that they ever belonged to 'Proletariat'. But Bardovsky was forced to acknowledge his authorship of the manifesto to officers, calling on them to rebel, since it was in his own hand-writing. It was of course a capital offence.

Waryński, Dulęba, Janowicz, Kunicki, Kon and a few others admitted that they were members of the party. Kunicki added that he was at the same time a member of 'Narodnaya Volya', and he expressed his party's and his own full solidarity with the Russian terrorist organisation. Waryński, too, when asked by a member of the prosecution, answered that he was in 'absolute solidarity' with 'Narodnaya Volya'.[7] Kunicki took the full responsibility for all projected and actual attacks on alleged police spies and agent-provocateurs during the ten months when he had been the leader of the party. He defended 'murder, which the party abhors', as forced on it by the government: 'One can only answer violence with violence', he said. Pacanowski and other witnesses for the prosecution repeated in open court (the hall was small and apart from those directly involved, only members of the accuseds' families were present during the trial) what they had said during the interrogatory stage. One of the advocates, Włodzimierz Spasowicz, a Pole, said during his very impressive plea that socialism and marxism were alien to Poles whose feelings were rather national than cosmopolitan; he added that it was not an accident that nearly all the leaders of 'Proletariat' had been brought up in Russian universities and had developed their 'subversive' ideas under the direct influence of Russian thought. Waryński decided to conduct his own defence.[8] He used this occasion, the last for him, publicly to develop his socialist-marxist ideas. He rejected the accusation that the party aimed at being a closed band of terrorists, and protested against the application of para. 249 of the criminal code, which foresaw only one punishment: death. 'We are not members of a sect, or dreamers detached from life.' He then enlarged on the way he saw capitalism developing in Europe, accompanied by misery for the industrial proletariat, which had to organise to defend its interests. He assured the court that the aim of the party he led was 'to move the workers clearly to understand their interests and to make them persevere in defending their rights'. He admitted that his party wanted to 'discipline and organise the working class and lead them in the struggle against the government and the privileged classes'. He then made clear his views on the Polish national question by saying: 'We are the enemies of the [Russian] government but we are not patriots in the political meaning of this word and we do not raise the national question. We are the enemies of the wealthy and privileged classes which in our country thanks to its evolution and political traditions are a powerful and dangerous opponent.'

He then went on to speak about the role of terror in his party's activities. He, like the whole party, he said, 'abhorred murder'. But the removal of spies and traitors he considered to be the natural right of every human group. As to political and economic terror, he defended it as the only weapon which in some circumstances the unjustly persecuted and oppressed could use against brutal men. In this connection he made two interesting remarks. The first was that it might be safer to channel the primitive passion for vengeance which could any minute erupt as a result of inhuman treatment of the poor into some organised form, and thus control and minimise its scope. On economic terror he said that it was always the result of the factory owners breaking the laws which protected their workers. He then gave the example of England where, he said, 'since . . . factory legislation was introduced and political freedom was enlarged and expanded to the workers, economic terrorism has stopped and the trade unions in England presently are under the protection of the law'. He ended his defence which had lasted more than an hour by saying: 'We do not stand above history, we comply with its laws. We consider the revolution, for which we aim, to be the consequence of historical evolution and of social conditions. We see it [the revolution] coming and strive not to meet it unprepared.'

Waryński's speech, according to contemporary reports, made a great impression on all present, among whom was General Hurko, the Governor-General of the Kingdom, by its clarity, evident honesty and courage.

Altogether twenty speeches for the defence were made during the trial. In their last words before sentence Waryński warned the judges that severe punishment could only result in even more brutality in the coming political and social struggle; Kunicki again expressed full solidarity with the Russian 'Narodnaya Volya' and accepted personal responsibility for the terrorist acts committed by members of 'Proletariat' on his orders. 'We will die in the certainty of having fulfilled our duty', he said.[9]

On 20 December the presiding judge announced the verdict:[10] Piotr Bardovsky, Stanisław Kunicki, Nicolai Lury, Michał Ossowski, Jan Pietrusiński and Józef Szmaus, were sentenced to death by hanging. Eighteen others, among whom was Waryński and the members of the party's Fighting Squad, were each sentenced to 16 years' hard labour. The traitor Pacanowski and 20-year-old Kon received 10 years 8 months' hard labour each. The two Russian officers, Ingelstrom and Sokolsky, were exiled for life to the remotest parts of Siberia. Not one of the accused was acquitted. The sentences had to be approved by the highest authorities in St Petersburg. The death sentences on Bardovsky, Kunicki, Ossowski and Pietrusiński were confirmed. The death sentences on Lury and Szmaus were commuted to twenty years' hard labour. Some of those who were sentenced to long terms of *Katorga* had their sentences slightly reduced, but not Waryński. Hurko, the Governor-General, tried in vain to persuade St Petersburg that the death sentences ought not to be carried out, because of the bad impression it would make on Polish society. He was supported in this by the chief of the gendarmerie. But a special council in the capital, and the Tsar personally, disagreed with these opinions.[11]

On 28 January 1886, at 7 o'clock in the morning, after having spent the night in separate cells with ministers of their faith, Kunicki, Bardovsky, Ossowski and Pietrusiński were hanged on the special gallows put up in the yard of the Tenth Pavilion of the Warsaw Citadel. These were the first political martyrs in the Kingdom since the 1863 uprising.

The rest were soon removed from the Warsaw prison. Waryński was locked up in the Shlisselburg fortress, the 'stone coffin', as this most dreaded political prison in Tsardom was known in Russia. He died there from consumption three years later, in February 1889, at the age of 33, still unbroken in spirit. Among those sent to the mines in Siberia, some committed suicide or died from exhaustion. Two prominent members of the party, Rechniewski and Kon, survived. Freed by the amnesty in 1905, they returned to Poland. They did not join the orthodox marxist SDKPiL (Social Democrats, of which Rosa Luxemburg was the most prominent leader), but the nationally-minded PPS.

The fifty-five members of 'Proletariat' arrested in the autumn of 1885 were dealt with differently. Only eighteen were kept in the Tenth Pavilion, while the rest were freed on bail. Some of them, together with Marian Stefan Ulrych who came from Geneva and was not known to the police, formed a new group of 'Proletariat' at the beginning of 1886. Their first task was to organise help for comrades in prison and for their families outside. The role of Piński, the 'leader' and agent-provocateur, at last became clear. Two members of the Ulrych group, a locksmith, Władysław Kowalewski, and a weaver, Victor Hipszer, decided to avenge a new wave of arrests, which started in the first days of April with the arrest of Ulrych and other members of the party.

They shot[12] the man they rightly considered to be the principal informant of the police three times on 1 July 1886, but the wounds were not serious. Six weeks later a military tribunal sentenced Kowalewski to death and Hipszer to life-long *Katorga*. On 4 September a lonely gallows again bore the body of a member of 'Proletariat'. There was no-one left outside to protest or even to mourn. 'Proletariat' was no more.

The last members of the party still on Polish soil were locked up in the grey-walled cells of the Tenth Pavilion. Their nerves were unbearably tense after the executions in January and September 1886. Even the most courageous could see no hope of a change in their fate after the final collapse of the organisation with the liquidation of the Ulrych group. In despair Bohuszewicz and others tried to assault Fursa, the governor of the prison. Eva Bresler, a seamstress born in Pińsk, hanged herself in her cell. The authorities decided to end the whole case without any publicity. No trial was held. Punishment was settled by the administration. Maria Bohuszewicz, Rozalia Felsenhardt, and nine other members of the group were sentenced to five years' exile each in eastern Siberia. Ten others were exiled for between three and four years. They were never to return to Poland. Many more were given short prison sentences. On 28 March 1888 the last of the Ulrych group was sentenced to ten years in eastern Siberia.[13] At the same time sentences were pronounced on members of the already non-existent party organisations in Łódź, Tomaszów and Zgierz. Again nine persons were sent to eastern or western Siberia.

Both young women, Bohuszewicz and Felsenhardt, died during the long and difficult journey to their places of exile. The toll which death took among the members of 'Proletariat' during their imprisonment and exile was very heavy. Some died because they could not bear the climate. Others broke down and committed suicide. Altogether over 300 persons were sentenced for belonging to 'Proletariat'.[14]

The leaders and members of the first Polish socialist party may have committed many imprudent acts, but they paid for them tenfold. Most of them met their cruel fate with admirable courage. In a nation where martyrs are saints, Waryński, Kunicki, Maria Bohuszewicz, though heretics, had established the socialist movement and its varied ideas as a respected part of Poland's history.

8 THE INHERITANCE

The reader of this account of the first Polish socialist party, indeed the first marxist organisation in Tsarist Russia, must be warned not to judge its ideas, or its practice, by the norms prevailing nine decades later. This is no sentimental appeal for tolerance for young men and women, all in their early twenties, who had to mature in a country ruled by a brutal autocracy. Even in much freer conditions they would still have had to go through the phases of trial-and-error of any pioneering movement. Even if they could have had easier access to the thought and ideas maturing and evolving in the rest of Europe, they would still have had to find out for themselves the needs, the interests, and the capacities of their own society, or parts of it.

That the leaders of the Social Revolutionary Party 'Proletariat' originated a serious movement in the life of contemporary Poland there can be no doubt. When less than ten years after the disappearance of 'Proletariat', two socialist parties, the patriotic PPS (Polish Socialist Party) and the orthodox marxist SDKPiL (Social Democratic Party of the Kingdom of Poland and Lithuania) were born, both claimed to be the heirs of 'Proletariat'. To this day any Polish Communist or Social Democrat looks back to the eighties of the last century as the time when the Polish labour movement was conceived and born.

However vehemently the founders of 'Proletariat' rejected Polish patriotism or refused to take part in the struggle for an independent state, objectively they brought into the national consciousness a new and growing group: yesterday's peasants who had only very recently migrated to the towns and industrial estates. It is true that Waryński and his friends talked only of classes. But a class is part of a bigger entity, of society and nation. In calling on the workers to organise themselves the socialists were destroying the workers' primary feeling of isolated personal existence. Appealing to them to fight against other groups and classes, the revolutionaries made them recognise existing social relationships. Thus national cohesion was born out of propaganda for unrelenting struggle. 'Proletariat' played a major role in bringing the Polish working class into the sphere of national politics long before this happened to the peasantry.

The last national uprising of 1863 closed the chapter during which the gentry were the acknowledged leaders of the nation. The possibility of no other class being found to take on this burden in the coming years constituted a real danger for the future existence of Polish society. For historical reasons there was no strong indigenous Polish bourgeoisie yet in existence. 'Proletariat' had begun the movement which had made it possible for a new national leadership, consisting of workers and a liberal-minded intelligentsia, to emerge. It was this alliance which formed the backbone of the movement for independence and social progress at the beginning of this century, and prepared the Poles for the rebirth of their country in the autumn of 1918.

An oppressed nation is a hating nation. After the many disasters in the second half of the nineteenth century the Poles detested the Russians, abhorred the Germans, and felt not much love for any other nation or race with which they were in daily contact. Whatever one may say about the distorting influence of general or particular hatred by a group, there can be no doubt that such emotions are the worst guide in politics for a nation, and especially for a country in Poland's geographical position.

'Proletariat' was the first popular movement in modern Polish history to look realistically for forces which could bring liberty to their society, and to state that this was possible only in an alliance with similar movements among the neighbouring and subjugating nations. The first Polish socialists overestimated the actual strength of the contemporary revolutionary movements. They expected miraculous changes to result from the desperate actions of a handful of Russian terrorists. But they were right in believing that it was nonsense to hope for a free Poland, when its neighbours, great or small, were enslaved. The selfishness and shortsightedness of chauvinism were alien to their way of thinking.

There was one other positive achievement of 'Proletariat'. There were many noble and sensitive men in Poland before Waryński, who felt deeply for those who lived a life of material and moral suffering. They wrote about it, they dreamed of reforms which would alleviate their harsh fate. But their attitude was that of patricians doing their duty to their helpless wards. In the second half of the nineteenth century this group had lost any politica and material power strong enough to serve as a lever for meaningful social and economic reforms. The new classes emerging as the result of a developing industrial society had to gain confidence in their own strength, and to find a place, and a purpose, in the nation. For the leaders of 'Proletariat' the marxist interpretation of history, however erroneous it may be, served well the need to give the working class of the new and growing industrial society a near mythical belief in their historical role as the begetters of a new order and as the future leaders of the nation.

'Proletariat' formed a bridge between the post-feudal, agricultural, gentry-led Poland and the emerging industrial, capitalist, socially reformist society. They were also pioneers of ideas of self-help, while at the same time boldly attacking the restraining narrow-mindedness of nationalism.

As we have seen in describing all the turns in the history of the eight years during which the first socialist party of the Poles was born, grew, and died, neither their ideas nor their actions followed a straight, well-thought-out and logical path. Rosa Luxemburg, who in 1893 became the most important leader of Polish marxism and remained so until her death in 1919, thought that 'from the moment of formalising the existence of the party . . . until its disappearance . . . it was permanently moving away [from the marxist position] in the direction of blanquism' (published in *Przeglad Socjaldemokratyczny* (1903), no. 1). Rosa Luxemburg saw Polish society as having to deal with the same problems which confronted the much more advanced nations of central and western Europe, and as having to follow the road mapped out for her generation by the founders of marxism. She never understood the deep national emotions which moved all parts of Polish society, and which at every turn rebelled against tidy schemes produced by overtly logical minds.

This should not be understood as a defence of everything 'Proletariat' did, or planned to do. Politically, the leaders of 'Proletariat' were utopians. They believed that the Social Revolution was just around the corner. They therefore never worked out any programme of the possible, or as the German Social Democrats called it, a minimum programme. While realistic about the limited use of terrorism at home they, especially in the second part of their short history, made themselves spiritual auxiliaries of Russian revolutionary terrorism, then already in its decaying phase. They talked about the immutable laws of human evolution, yet their millennial dreams impelled them to be impatient, and sometimes even violent when history would not move as fast as they wished.

Like all pioneers they were often intolerant. By their extreme anti-patriotism they unnecessarily made enemies of potential friends, and thus prepared the split in the future Polish labour movement.

Yet when after the executions in January 1886 those who were sentenced to *Katorga* wrote in their collective letter addressed to those few of their comrades who were still free: 'Do not let this cause perish', they saw the future more clearly than their oppressors.

NOTES

CHAPTER I: THE DEFEATED PAST

1. *The Cambridge history of Poland*, vol. II, *1697–1935*, p. 378.
2. F. Perl (Res), *Dzieje ruchu socjalistycznego w zaborze rosyjskim do powstania P.P.S.* (Warsaw, 1958), p. 45.
3. W. Feldman, *Geschichte der politischen Ideen in Polen seit dessen Teilungen (1795–1914)* (Munich and Berlin, 1917), p. 214.
4. J. Grabiec, *Dzieje narodu polskiego* (Cracow, 1909), p. 331.
5. *Cambridge history of Poland*, II, 383.
6. Grabicc, *op. cit.*, p. 331.
7. W. Tokarz, *Kraków w początkach powstania styczniowego i wyprawa na Miechów* (Cracow, 1914), II, 153–5 and 211–13, quoted in R. F. Leslie, *Reform and insurrection in Russian Poland 1856–1865* (London, 1963).
8. Dr Edmund Brzeziński, 'Wspomnienia z mojego życia' in *Niepodległość* (1933), vol. 4, part 7, pp. 49–50.
9. *Cambridge history of Poland*, II, 388.
10. I. Kostrowicka, Z. Landau, J. Tomaszewski, *Historia gospodarcza Polski XIX i XX wieku* (Warsaw, 1966), p. 191.
11. *Ibid.* pp. 147–51.
12. *Memorandum* dated 16 January 1882, reproduced from original in N. Gąsiorowska-Grabowska (ed.), *Źródła do dziejów klasy robotniczej na ziemiach polskich 1864–1914* (Warsaw, 1962), I, 112–13.
13. On Christmas Day, 25 and 26 December 1881, a mob attacked Jewish-owned stores in Warsaw. Some 850 of them were looted and destroyed, see *Źródła*, I, 113.
14. I. Kostrowicka *et al.*, *Historia*, p. 190.
15. *Ibid.* p. 187.
16. Marian Kukiel, *Dzieje Polski porozbiorowej (1795–1921)* (London, 1961), p. 400. See also *Report* of Warsaw Governor, Lieutenant-General N. N. Medem, to the Tsar (1880) in *Źródła*, pp. 89–93.
17. St A. Kempner, *Rozwój gospodarczy Polski od rozbiorów do niepodległośći* (Warsaw, 1924), pp. 85 and 104.
18. Janusz Durko, 'Klasa robotnicza w dobie działalności "Proletariatu"', in *Z Pola Walki* (Warsaw, 1963), no. 1–2, p. 56.
19. Informator, *Stronnictwa polityczne w Królestwie Polskim* (Cracow, no date), p. 4.
20. M. Kukiel, *Dzieje Polski porozbiorowej*, pp. 384–5.
21. *Ibid.* p. 389.
22. *Ibid.* p. 387.
23. P. Popiel, *Pisma* (Cracow, 1893), I, 72.

24. Aleksander Świętochowski, *Wskazania polityczne* (Warsaw, 1888), p. 54.
25. B. Bolesławita (J. Kraszewski), *Z roku 1863 rachunki* (Poznań, 1868), pp. 21–2, as quoted in A. Bromke's *Poland's politics: idealism versus realism* (Cambridge, Mass., 1967).
26. M. Kukiel, *Dzieje Polski porozbiorowej*, p. 393.
27. Ludwik Krzywicki, *Wspomnienia*, vol. II (Warsaw, 1958), pp. 270–1.
28. A. Świętochowski, *Socjalizm i jego błędy* (Nowiny, Warsaw, 20 October 1878). Quoted in L. Baumgarten, *Dzieje Wielkiego Proletariatu* (Warsaw, 1966), p. 75.

CHAPTER 2 A NEW GENERATION

1. Perl, *Dzieje ruchu socjalistycznego*, p. 51.
2. A. Próchnik, *Studia z dziejów polskiego ruchu robotniczego* (Warsaw, 1958), p. 44.
3. L. Krzywicki, *Wspomnienia*, II, 63.
4. F. Kon, *Za piadysiat lyet* (Moscow, 1935). Reprinted in *Wspomnienia o Proletariacie* (Warsaw, 1953), pp. 105–6.
5. A. Próchnik, *Studia z dziejów polskiego ruchu robotniczego*, pp. 51–2.
6. In *Na Rodinye* (London (Geneva), N.T., 1882), quoted in S. Volk's *Narodnaya Volya 1879–1882* (Moscow–Leningrad, 1966), p. 404.
7. Byloye (London, 1903), p. 194.
8. Perl, *Dzieje ruchu socjalistycznego*, p. 49.
9. L. Baumgarten, *Dzieje Wielkiego Proletariatu*, pp. 167–8.
10. F. Gross, *The Polish worker: a study of a social stratum* (New York, 1944), p. 111.
11. Próchnik, *Studia z dziejów polskiego ruchu robotniczego*, pp. 31–54, also T. Daniszewski, *Wielki Proletariat* (Warsaw, 1951), pp. 11–14; and L. Krzywicki, *Wspomnienia*, II, 76–85.
12. Dr E. Brzeziński, 'Wspomnienia z mojego żyćia', p. 57.
13. Rosa Luxemburg (in an article published in *Przegląd Socjaldemokratyczny* (1903), nos. 1 and 2) accuses the 'Proletariat' leadership of the second period of having abandoned its clear marxist ideology.

CHAPTER 3: THE BEGINNING

1. L. Krzywicki, *Wspomnienia*, II, 83.
2. Kazimierz Dłuski (Na-Z): 'Ludwik Waryński (osobiste wspomnienia)', in *Z Pola Walki* (London, 1904), pp. 43–50.
3. Amerikanin (J. Uziembło): 'Wspomnienia z 1878 roku', in *ibid.* pp. 51–4.
4. K. Dłuski, *op. cit.*
5. Próchnik, *Studia z dziejów polskiego ruchu robotniczego*, p. 17.
6. Baumgarten, *Dzieje Wielkiego Proletariatu*, p. 11.
7. *Równość* (Geneva, 1 October 1878), pp. 1–5.
8. Uziembło, 'Wspomnienia z 1878 roku'.
9. *Ibid.*
10. Próchnik, 'Pierwszy sad wojenny', in *Kronika ruchu rewolucyjnego w Polsce* (Warsaw, 1935), no. 1.

L

11. *Źródła*, I, 66–7.
12. Quoted by A. Próchnik, *op. cit.*
13. *Z Pola Walki* (Geneva, 1886), pp. 23–4.
14. T. Daniszewski, *Wielki Proletariat*, p. 37.
15. Barbara Szerer in *Z Pola Walki* (Warsaw, 1963), no. 1–2, pp. 198–9.
16. Daniszewski, *op. cit.*, p. 46; see also *Z Pola Walki, ibid.* p. 22.
17. Perl, *Dzieje ruchu socjalistycznego*, p. 117.
18. See, e.g., the speech by Bolesław Bierut at the unifying congress of the Polish United Workers' Party in December 1948 in Warsaw, reprinted in Daniszewski, *op. cit.*, pp. viii–xi.
19. *Marks i Engels o Polsce, Zbiór materiałów* (Warsaw, 1960), II, 103–4.
20. *Ibid.* pp. 118–21.
21. *Równość* (Geneva, November 1880), no. 1, pp. 1–5.
22. *Niepodległość* (1930), I, 341–4: see also Bolesław Limanowski, *Pamiętniki (1870–1907)* (Warsaw, 1957), II, 265–71.
23. *Sprawozdanie z międzynarodowego zebrania, zwołanego w pięćdziesiątą rocznicę powstania listopodawego*, Bibl. Równość (Geneva, 1881), I, 30–3; see also Perl, *Dzieje ruchu socjalistycznego*, pp. 122–4.
24. *Sprawozdanie*, p. 6.
25. Lev Deich, 'Pionerzy ruchu socjalistycznego w Królestwie Polskim' in *Z Pola Walki* (Moscow, 1930), nos. 9–10, reprinted in *Wspomnienia o Proletariacie*, pp. 30–1.
26. Deich, *op. cit.*, pp. 27–31.
27. *Przedświt* (Geneva, 1881), nos. 7 and 8.
28. Deich, *op. cit.*, pp. 32–3.

CHAPTER 4: A PARTY OF MARXIST REVOLUTIONARIES

1. Krzywicki, *Wspomnienia*, II, 132–3 and 231–5.
2. *Przedświt* (1882), nos. 1–2.
3. The only surviving copy of this leaflet is in the possession of the Central Historical Archive in Leningrad. It is photographically reproduced in Baumgarten, *Dzieje Wielkiego Proletariatu*, pp. 108–9.
4. *Proletariat, organ Międzynarodowej Socjalno-Rewolucyjnej Partii* (Warsaw), No. 1, 15 września (September) 1883. Only one full set has survived, which is now in the possession of the Marx-Engels-Lenin Institute in Moscow. In 1957 a re-edition of all five issues of *Proletariat* was published, from photostats, in Warsaw under the title: *Proletariat, 1883–84*. All further quotations from this periodical will be taken from the Warsaw re-edition, pp. 114 + xxvi.
5. Protocol of police investigation on 24 December 1884 (old style) quoted in Baumgarten, *op. cit.*, p. 114.
6. It was republished in *Przedświt* on 17 October 1882 and with some omissions in *Z Pola Walki* (1886), pp. 54–6.
7. Baumgarten, *op. cit.*, pp. 121–2, and Próchnik, *Studia z dziejów polskiego ruchu robotniczego*, pp. 247–8.
8. Georgy Plekhanov, *Nachalo robotchego dvizhenia*, p. 234, as quoted in *Z Pola Walki* (1963), nos. 1–2, p. 147.

9. 'Z Archiwum Piotra Bardowskiego', *Z Pola Walki* (Warsaw, 1960), no. 1, pp. 98–9.
10. Baumgarten, *op. cit.*, pp. 127–32.
11. The leaflet was also published in the party's Geneva periodical *Przedświt* (no. 10, 20 January 1883) giving its date of publication in Warsaw as 21 December 1882. It should have been 31 December.
12. *Przedświt* (April 1883), no. 15, and also in *Z Pola Walki* (1886), pp. 37–8.
13. *Ibid.*
14. Baumgarten, *op. cit.*, p. 166.
15. Krzywicki, *Wspomnienia*, 1, 238–64.
16. Description of the strike by a contemporary (article unsigned) in *Z Pola Walki* (London, 1904), pp. 125–8.
17. 'Strajk żyrardowski (23–8 IV 1883) w dokumentach władz carskich.' *Z Pola Walki* (Warsaw, 1958), no. 3, p. 111.
18. Baumgarten, *op. cit.*, p. 144.
19. *Przedświt* (14 May 1883), no. 17, p. 2.
20. *Ibid.*
21. *Ibid.* (10 January 1883), no. 9, p. 2.
22. *Ibid.* (14 May 1883), no. 17.

CHAPTER 5: TIME OF SUCCESS

1. *Przedświt* (15 July 1883), no. 22.
2. As quoted in Baumgarten, *Dzieje Wielkiego Proletariatu.* p. 238.
3. Żanna Kormanowa, 'Proletariat' – dzieje, historiografia' in *Z Pola Walki* (1963), no. 1–2, p. 21.
4. *Przedświt* (22 June 1883), no. 20.
5. See Kon, *Wspomnienia o Proletariacie*, pp. (in Polish edition) 59–64.
6. Baumgarten, *op. cit.*, pp. 181 ff.
7. Próchnik, 'Działalność wydawnicza Proletariatu' in *Kronika ruchu rewolucyjnego w Polsce* (1936), no. 1.
8. *Ibid.*
9. Hilary (Gostkiewicz), 'Wspomnienia proletariatczyka' in *Z Pola Walki* (Moscow, 1927), no. 2.
10. *Proletariat, 1883–84*, pp. 4–5.
11. Próchnik, *op. cit.*
12. *Z Pola Walki* (Moscow, 1927), no. 1.
13. Feliks Kon, who took part in printing *Proletariat* and wrote for it, gives the round figure of 3,000 copies as the average edition of each of the five issues which appeared in 1883 and 1884 in Warsaw (Feliks Kon, *Sorok lyet pod znamenyem revolutsii* (Moscow–Petrograd, no date), p. 34).
14. Próchnik, *op. cit.*, p. 269.
15. Hilary, *op. cit.*

CHAPTER 6: TIME OF TERROR

1. *Z Pola Walki* (1886), pp. 48–9.

2. Baumgarten, *Dzieje Wielkiego Proletariatu*, pp. 283–5.
3. See *Kronika*, report of arrests, published in third issue of *Proletariat* (20 October 1883), pp. 35–6 (re-edition).
4. *Kronika ruchu rewolucyjnego* (1936), no. 1.
5. Kon, *Sorok lyepod znamenyem revolutsii*, p. 24.
6. *Ibid.* p. 124.
7. *Ibid.* p. 128.
8. *Ibid.* p. 24. In an article written by Kunicki for the sixth issue of the Warsaw periodical, which was seized by the police in Bardovsky's flat in July 1884, he based his hopes of winning the Polish peasantry for the cause of the revolution on the fantastic assertion that there is alive in the villages a tradition of common ownership of the land ('Z Archiwum Bardowskiego' in *Z Pola Walki* (1960), no. 1, p. 95).
9. 'Kronika', in *Proletariat* (May 1884), no. 5, p. 66.
10. 'Special Communiqué', in *Proletariat* (20 October 1883), no. 3, pp. 34–5.
11. 'Special Communiqué', in *Proletariat* (20 November 1883), no. 4, pp. 47–8.
12. *Wielki Proletariat, op. cit.*, pp. 131–2.
13. *Z Pola Walki* (1886), pp. 121–4.
14. Daniszewski, *Wielki Proletariat*, pp. 183–7. The document itself was in all probability written abroad after Kunicki met the group of his political friends who were then living in Geneva and Paris.
15. *Walka Klas* (Geneva 1884), no. 4, pp. 4–6.
16. *Wielki Proletariat*, pp. 179–82. The only existing copy of the Agreement was made by the police and attached to the acts of the trial of the 29 members of the party which took place in Warsaw in December 1885. It is kept in the Soviet archives in Moscow.
17. The Polish text was printed in *Walka Klas* (Geneva, September 1884), no. 6; the Russian text appeared in no. 10 of *Narodnaya Volya* (September 1884).
18. A. Próchnik, 'Początki polskiej propagandy socjalistycznej w Poznaniu zepokiustaw wyjątkowych przeciw socjalistom' in *Niepodległość* (Warsaw, 1935), vol. 11, parts 1 and 2.
19. 'Prospect' of *Walka Klas*, quoted in Baumgarten, *Dzieje Wielkiego Proletariatu*, p. 361.
20. Res (Perl), *Dzieje ruchu socjalistycznego*, p. 198.
21. Żanna Kormanowa, 'Kazimierz Puchewicz i Solidarność' in *Niepodległość* (1935), vol. 19, part 1, pp. 1–27.
22. *Proletariat* (1 October 1883), no. 2, p. 21.
23. 'Z Archiwum Bardowskiego', *Z Pola Walki* (1960), no. 1, pp. 106–7.
24. *Z Pola Walki* (1886), p. 116.
25. *Proletariat* (May 1884), no. 5, p. 72.
26. *Z Pola Walki* (1886), p. 50.
27. L. Baumgarten (ed.), *Kółka socjalistyczne, Gminy i Wielki Proletariat. Procesy polityczne 1878–1888* (Warsaw, 1966), p. 409.
28. Daniszewski, *Wielki Proletariat*, pp. 162–3.
29. 'Z Archiwum Bardowskiego', in *Z Pola Walki* (1959), no. 3, pp. 93–108.
30. *Z Pola Walki* (1886), pp. 116–17.

31. *Ibid.* pp. 112–15.
32. Kon, *Sorok lyet pod znamenyem revolutsii*, pp. 3–4.
33. *Kółka*, pp. 694 and 704.
34. I. Orczak, 'Dzialalność serbskiego rewolucjonisty Andre Bankowicza' in *Z Pola Walki* (1959), no. 3, pp. 57 ff.
35. Baumgarten, *Dzieje Wielkiego Proletariatu*, p. 569.
36. *Ibid.* pp. 576–9.
37. *Kółka*, p. 843.
38. *Ibid.* pp. 902–4.
39. *Z Pola Walki* (1886), p. 59.

CHAPTER 7: THE GOVERNMENT'S REVENGE

1. Perl, *Dzieje ruchu socjalistycznego*, pp. 182–3.
2. *Vollman Archiv*, Internationaal Instituut voor Sociale Geschiedenis, Amsterdam.
3. *Z Pola Walki*, (1886), pp. 62–3.
4. Baumgarten, *op. cit.*, p. 543.
5. *Ibid.* pp. 546–9.
6. Mrs E. L. Woynicz, letter to the Deputy Librarian, London School of Economics and Political Science, Woynicz Collection at the British Library of Political and Economic Science.
7. *Z Pola Walki* (1886), pp. 88–91.
8. *Ibid.* pp. 145–53.
9. *Ibid.* pp. 155–7.
10. *Ibid.* pp. 45–8, see also *Źródła*, vol. I, part 1, pp. 155–7.
11. Baumgarten, *op. cit.*, pp. 677–9.
12. A. Próchnik, 'Piąta szubienica' in *Kronika ruchu rewolucyjnego w Polsce* (1935). See full text of sentence in *Źródła*, I, 172–7.
13. *Źródła*, I, 183–5.
14. *Ibid.* pp. 199–200.

BIBLIOGRAPHY

Archiv Zemlyi i Volyi i Narodnoy Volyi, Moscow, 1932.
Baumgarten, L. *Dzieje Wielkiego Proletariatu*, Warsaw, 1966.
(editor) *Kółka socjalistyczne, Gminy i Wielki Proletariat. Procesy polityczne 1878–1888*, Warsaw, 1966.
Bazyłow, L. *Działalność narodnictwa rosyjakiego w latach 1878–1881*, Wrocław, 1960.
Bicz, H. (editor). *Proletariat, pierwsza socjalno-rewolucyjna partia w Polsce*, Moscow, 1934.
Bohuszewiczówna, M. *Pamiętniki*, Wrocław, 1955.
Buszko, J. *Narodziny ruchu socjalistycznego na ziemiach polskich*, Cracow, 1967.
The Cambridge history of Poland, vol. II, Cambridge, 1941.
Daniszewski, T. (editor). *Wielki Proletariat*, Warsaw, 1951.
Dziewanowski, M. K. *The Communist Party of Poland*, Cambridge, Mass., 1959.
Falkowski, M. and Kowalik, T. *Początki marksistowskiej myśli ekonomicznej w Polace. Wybór publicystyki z lat 1880–1885*, Warsaw, 1957.
Feldman, W. *Dzieje polskiej mysli politycznej*, Cracow-Warsaw, 1920.
Geschichte der politischen Ideen in Polen seit dessen Teilungen (1795–1914), Munich and Berlin, 1917.
Gąsiorowska-Grabowska, Natalia (editor). *Źródła do dziejów klasy robotniczej na ziemiach polskich 1864–1914*, 3 volumes (to date), Warsaw, 1962 and 1968.
Grabiec, J. *Dzieje narodu polskiego*, Cracow, 1909.
Gross, F. *The Polish worker: a study of a social stratum*, New York, 1944.
Gruenberg, K. and Kozłowski, Cz. *Historia polskiego ruchu robotniczego, 1864–1918*, Warsaw, 1962.
Halstein, U. *Sozialismus und nationale Frage in Polen*, Cologne-Vienna, 1969.
Informator, Stronnictwa polityczne w Królestwie Polskim, Cracow, no date.
Itenberg, B. C. and Volk, S. S. (editors). *Revolutsionneye narodnichestvo*, 2 volumes, Moscow, 1965.
Katorga i Ssilka (periodical), Moscow, 1926.
Kempner, St A. *Rozwój gospodarczy Polski od rozbiorów do niepodległości*, Warsaw, 1924.
Kon, F. *Pod sztandarem rewolucji*, Warsaw, 1959.
Sorok lyet pod znamenem revolutsii, Moscow-Petrograd, no date.
'Proletariat', Moscow, 1931.
Kormanowa, Ź. *Materiały do bibliografii druków socjalistycznych na ziemiach polskich w latach 1866–1918*, Warsaw, 1935.

Korzec, P. *Wielki Proletariat w okręgu łódzkim*, Łódź, 1963.

Kostrowicka, I., Landau, Z. and Tomaszewski, J. *Historia gospodarcza Polski XIX i XX wieku*, Warsaw, 1966.

Koszutski, S. *Rozwój ekonomiczny Królestwa Polskiego w ostatnim trzydzie-stuleciu (1870–1900)*, Warsaw, 1905.

Kronika ruchu rewolucyjnego w Polsce (periodical), Warsaw, 1936–9.

Krzywicki, L. *Wspomnienia*, 3 volumes, Warsaw, 1957–9.

Kukiel, M. *Dzieje Polski porozbiorowej (1795–1921)*, London, 1961.

Leslie, R. F. *Reform and insurrection in Russian Poland 1856–1865*, London, 1963.

Limanowski, B. *Pamiętniki (1835–1870 and 1907–1919)*, Warsaw, 1957. *Historia demokracji polskiej w epoce porozbiorowej*, Warsaw, 1957.

Luxemburg, R. *Die industrielle Entwicklung Polens*, Leipzig, 1898.

Marx, K. *Manuskripte ueber die polnische Frage*, 's-Gravenhage, 1961.

Marx i Engels o Polsce, Zbiór materiałów, Warsaw, 1960.

Mazowiecki, M. *Historia ruchu socjalistycznego w zaborze rosyjskim*, Cracow, 1903.

Molska, A. *Pierwsze pokolenie marksistów polskich 1878–1888*, Warsaw, 1962.

Niepodległość (periodical), 1930 onwards.

Perl, F. (Res) *Dzieje ruchu socjalistycznego w zaborze rosyjskim do powstania P.P.S.*, Warsaw, 1958.

Pobóg-Malinowski, W. *Najnowsza historia polityczna Polski*, London, 1960.

Próchnik, A. *Studia z dziejów polskiego ruchu robotniczego*, Warsaw, 1958.

Proletariat, organ Międzynarodowej Socjalno-Rewolucyjnej Partii (Warszawa 1883–1884), Recdycja, Warsaw, 1957.

Przedświt 1881–1886 (periodical), Geneva.

Równość 1879–1881 (periodical), Geneva.

Snitko, T. G. *Ruskoye narodnichestvo i polskoye obshchetsvennoye dvizhenye 1865–1881*, Moscow, 1969.

Sprawozdanie z międzynarodowego zebrania, zwołanego w 50-letnią rocznicę listapodowego powstania przez redakcję 'Równości' w Genewie, Geneva, 1881.

Strobel, G. W. *Quellen zur Geschichte des Kommunismus in Polen 1878–1918*, Cologne, 1968.

Świętochowski, A. *Wskazania polityczne*, Warsaw, 1888.

Volk, S. S. *Narodnaya Volya 1879–1882*, Moscow–Leningrad, 1966.

Volkovitcher, I. *Natchalo polskogo socialisticheskogo rabochego dvizhenia v' bioshey ruskoy Polshi*, Moscow–Leningrad, 1925.

Walka Klas 1884–1887 (perodical), Geneva.

Wawrykowa, M. *Rewolucyjne narodnictwo w latach siedemdziesiątych XIX wieku*, Warsaw, 1963.

Wspomnienia o Proletariacie, Warsaw, 1953.

Z dziejów współpracy rewolucyjnej Polaków i Rosjan w drugiej połowie XIX wieku, Wrocław, 1956.

Z Pola Walki, Geneva, 1886.

London, 1904.

(periodical), Warsaw since 1957.

INDEX